CATCH ME OR KILL ME

CATCH ME OR KILL ME

BY SUSAN PARROTT

This book is based on a true story. The names have been changed
to protect the innocent and the guilty. Whether the stories I
was told by my father's family, friends, bank robbing partners,
attorneys and victims are true or not, I need to tell them.

CATCH ME OR KILL ME
Copyright © 2022 by Susan Parrott

Bull riding photograph on the cover courtesy of Larry Wyche.
Motorcycle photograph on the cover courtesy of Dan Mahony.

ISBN 979-8-9863370-0-5 (Hardcover)
ISBN 979-8-9863370-1-2 (Paperback)
ISBN 979-8-9863370-2-9 (eBook)

For Charles Lee and Toni

ACKNOWLEDGEMENTS

I'd like to thank the late Jim Hatfield for prompting me to write this book in 2014. If not for Jim, I would have never taken on this journey. He got the ball rolling by introducing me to Lyndall "Zoom Zoom" Brown. Zoom Zoom has been incredibly supportive through this process and has been on my team for the last eight years.

I will forever be grateful to Jim Strange. His recollection of the past led me to all the key players, bank robberies, and fascinating stories, which were unveiled though twenty hours of interviews. He became friends with Charles when they were thirteen and no one knew Charles better than he did.

I'd also like to thank Nancy Scuri. She is my rock. She spent countless hours editing and coaching me throughout the development of this manuscript. I also owe a big thank you to Michelle Taft Morris for introducing us.

Amy Wilson is a wonderful lady. I am grateful to her for coaching me on the second manuscript of the book. Which I fully intend to release as a follow up to this volume. Amy gave me courage and inspired me to be a better writer.

A special thanks goes to Patsy Beck Peirce, Charles's second wife. She gave the insight of a woman who loved my father deeply. Her children, Robyn Rhodes Axton, Rickey Rhodes, and Jason Peirce provided wonderful stories about the experiences of their life with Charles.

One of my best interviews was with the late Billy Ray Holloway. He was a young lawyer who assisted in representing

Charles in court and developed a friendship with him. His stories made me laugh and cry. He was there for my father throughout his life. A true friend.

My interviews with the following people assisted me in the building the book. And I thank those whose names I do not reveal as they requested to remain anonymous. Without them, I couldn't have properly told the many stories of Charles Parrott's life:

Charlie Neale	Larry and Lou Jean Wyche
Kelly Parker	Yvonne Garcia
Donald White	Geneva Shults
Caroline Ketcher-Horn	Lester Yocum
Bob and Pat Leatherwood	Archie Steele
Delores Hargrove	Elaine Warren

Thanks as well to the following people who helped me along the way:

Stacy Wyche	Tracy Wyche
Charlene Neale	Earline Dixon
Marla Cantrell	Tom Wing
Steve Garrett	Jacklyn Perry Ryan
Carolyn Thompson	Patty Ferry

I am grateful to Marilyn Friedman and Jeff Bernstein, the founders of the Writing Pad in Los Angeles, California. I always felt heard while taking classes with authors Jennifer Brody, Gretchen McNeil, and editor Trish Daly, and I had wonderful support from all my classmates.

Bull riding picture on the cover courtesy of Larry Wyche and the Motorcycle picture on the cover courtesy of Dan Mahony.

CONTENTS

Foreword 1

Double Cross 3

Becoming a Bank Robber 15

Goodbye Big City 25

Vian, Oklahoma 31

The Bull riders 38

On His Own 43

Slim James 50

Gracemont 66

Mccurtain County 85

French And Mcglinty 105

The Best Attorney That Money Can Buy 118

Rat Finks 126

All Hell Is Breaking Loose 148

Justice For Charles 178

The Submarine Getaway 187

Counting Bullets 194

Alaska 199

The Hat on the Bed 209

Patsy 221

Hartford 229

Out On Bond 246

The Burn Bar 262

The Big House 276

FOREWORD

There's something about the Cookson Hills and outlaws. These hills and hollers have produced noted figures with a complex relationship with the law—Zeke Proctor, Ned Christie, Charles "Pretty Boy" Floyd to name just a few. And add to that list Charles Parrott. Charles Parrott and I share a hometown, Stilwell, Oklahoma, located right in the heart of the Cookson Hills. Although we were separated by a generation, the world in which we both grew up was similar. Stilwell was the quintessential all-American town, as much as any other town could claim, with its railroad depot, one newspaper, family-owned stores lining Division Street, with modest houses and farms populated by hardworking folks. It was also unlike most towns in America. More Cherokee Indians lived in and around Stilwell than anywhere else in the nation, making the culture unique in that little section of the world. The area is one of the more impoverished communities in the United States and was even more so in the days of Charles's youth. The rugged terrain makes progress and development difficult. In Stilwell, lines blurred. While America was balanced between tradition and the space age, the folks in Stilwell practiced a form of Ozarks pragmatism. Folks in the Cookson Hills were no strangers to keeping a foot in more than one camp. Whether it be spanning the divide between Native American heritage and certain privileges coming easier by identifying as White, dealing daily with those who were more than well off and those that lived near destitution, the line between law abider and law breaker was indeed blurry. It was not uncommon for a respected farmer to secretly (and sometimes not-so-secretly) operate a still. Or a well-thought-of mother could raise America's most prolific bank robber. This blurry world, where Zeke Proctor, Ned Christie and "Pretty Boy" Floyd were recognized as desperate criminals but were also hailed as heroes, is where Charles Parrott came of age.

His outlaw career demonstrated his understanding of that balancing act between the traditional and the new. He counted on the sleepy natures of small towns, the laxness of local banks, and unprepared law enforcement. His bank jobs were researched and well-rehearsed, making the most of brazenness and misdirection. When I was a lad, it was generally agreed that Charles's poor choice to be on the wrong side of the law was something that shouldn't be discussed. But when it was discussed, usually in whispers or in safe company, there was a pride expressed that, even though it was wrong, one of our own had risen to the top of his field. The lines were still blurry … But now Charles's daughter can tell his story, the how and why of what made a small-town boy go rogue and why he was so good at it. Once it was a story not to be discussed in polite circles, but it is a story with a certain depth. It is a story that needs to be told.

  – Steve Garrett, historian, writer, and host of the
  Within the Realm podcast

DOUBLE CROSS

Charles was on his weekly whisky run to Pineville, Missouri. He gripped the steering wheel tightly, as the violent Oklahoma winds were forcing his customized car, a 1949 Nash Super 600, to swerve on the two-lane highway. He was proud of the fact that he'd been driving this car for the last two years and hadn't wrecked it. He had dusted out some cops a couple of weeks ago, and he was sure he was going to lose it on a gravel road, but he'd managed to regain control.

He was an expert at the 180. If he couldn't shake the cops, he would spin the car 180 degrees and quickly change direction and fly right past the lawman going in the opposite direction. This was a favorite move of his. He loved seeing the face of the officer as he flew past him. The car had specialized shocks to hold the seven hundred pounds of the extra weight of the liquor. The rear car seat of the Nash came with a factory mattress to make the rear seat into a double bed. That area was customized to make more room for the liquor. Charles had a switch that would extinguish the brake and taillights to throw off the cops while he made a turn or found a good hiding place.

It was April of 1958, and Oklahoma was one of the only states that still prohibited the sale of liquor. Bootleggers traveled to neighboring states to pick up the load and sold it for double the cost. There was a lot of money to be made, and Charles was enjoying the fruits of his labor and the fast lifestyle that came with it.

Today, he was running an hour early, so he could stop in to see his old friend, Don Delow. Don was a small man with dark slicked-back hair, and he had a big personality that made up for his small stature. He had been good friends to him since he was thirteen and Don was sixteen. Charles had always looked up to Don and considered him to be his oldest and closest friend. He also helped Charles to get his job with Mr. Jay Chaney, one of the Oklahoma City kingpins of the bootleggers.

He arrived at Don's around seven o'clock that evening. As he opened the car door, he heard a low growl. He swung back into the car and then he saw the pit bull tied to the nearby tree and another tied up by a doghouse. Charles stepped out of the car and walked toward the poor devil. He had a fondness for dogs but as he approached, the big beast lunged toward him, teeth bared. He heard the crack of a branch on the tree as the dog lunged again, pulling hard against its chain. Charles turned and bounded up the steps two at a time up to the porch.

A young blonde opened the door as he hit the top step. She smelled like a candy store. She had long blonde hair falling over her shoulders, and she was wearing a flimsy white shirt that revealed her curvy body.

"You must be Charlie. These boys have been telling me all about how wild you are."

"They're liars. Don't believe them," he said with a chuckle.

"I'm Josie. You sure seem nice for a bootlegger." She ran her hand up the front of his suit then grabbed his arm and pulled him inside the cabin.

Don was sitting at the table smoking a cigar and drinking whisky with his cousin, Melvin. Bo Diddley was singing "Pretty Thing" on the record player.

"You good-looking son of a bitch. How are you?" said Don.

"I'm good and thirsty. You got a soda pop?"

"Ah shit, you still following the rules of no drinking on the job?"

"Yeah, man. It keeps me straight."

Melvin nodded to Charles and extended his hand to him. Charles grabbed his wet slippery hand and felt uneasy, wiping his hand on his pants.

"Josie, get Charlie a 7 Up and don't spike it," said Don. "I may have gotten fired from running liquor for Chaney, but I'm making a good living running whisky to Tulsa."

Charles said, "You're lucky that your sister married the kingpin. That opened the door for you and me to get our jobs with him."

"My sister tried to stick up for me, but Chaney wouldn't give. He never liked me."

"Looks like you got a good setup here on the border. Close to the pick-up spot and convenient for me to stop in and see you more often, but your dogs scared me. You're going have to introduce me, so I don't get attacked."

"Gotta have 'em to protect the merchandise. Melvin, go feed those dogs and bring one in to meet Charlie."

Melvin went out the door and returned with one of the dogs. She was a solid deep gray with piercing eyes named Sheba. Don handed Charles a can of Vienna sausage and he opened it to feed her. He had her eating out of his hand and licking his face immediately.

"I just got this magazine with some good-looking hot rods I wanted to show you. You and I need to get back on the racetrack." Don opened the magazine and handed it to Charles. Charles smiled as he looked through the magazine. He did miss racing cars and motorcycles.

Don turned the volume up on the record player as Bo Diddley was going into his solo. He had told Josie beforehand to distract Charles once he turned up the volume. She did as she was told, and she liked the looks of him. He was tall with gold flecked, hazel eyes and dark hair.

Charles said, "You got yourself a flirtatious little filly, but I'm not biting."

He missed his best friend from childhood, and if his wife knew he was here, she would be mad. She'd never liked Don. After a half hour had passed, he left the cabin with an urgency in his step. He did not want to be late to pick up of his liquor.

Charles pulled into the pick-up spot just outside of Pineville. The delivery driver wasn't there yet. He reached down to pull the money bag out of the hidden compartment, but his hand grasped at air. The bag was gone.

"Damn that Don Delow!" he roared.

He fumbled around in vain, looking for the bag while knowing he wouldn't find it. Don was a con artist to the core. Gripping the wheel, Charles tried to think. *What am I going to do?* He'd been lured to the cabin by the river. Don hadn't seized an opportunity; he had planned this.

As Charles was sitting there steaming about the situation, the drop man pulled up. Charles knew he had to be cool. He was in big trouble, and it wouldn't pay to panic. He jumped out of the car and walked straight up to the window of the big panel wagon before Jeff, the drop man, could get out.

"Jeff, you ain't gonna believe it! I left the money bag back in Oklahoma City! I gotta turn around and go right back. Can I meet you back here tomorrow evening?"

"I don't know, Charlie. I have three runs tomorrow. And it's a real pisser that I have to unload and reload your whisky."

"How about I give you an extra hundred for your trouble?"

"It's a deal. It will have to be late, though. Eight again tomorrow night? And don't be late."

Back at the cabin, Melvin and Don discussed what had taken place. While Charles had been occupied with the dog and the magazine, Don had sent Melvin out to the car to get the money bag. Don knew all the tricks. Hell, he had taught Charles everything he knew, so Melvin didn't even have to hunt for the bag. Don had told him right where it would be. He had also told Melvin to put the bag in the doghouse of the meanest dog they had.

"Why are you doing this to Charlie?" Melvin asked.

"I want to get back at Chaney for firing me. And because I can."

"You're just going to get Charlie in a whole mess of trouble."

"Yeah, well maybe Charlie will have to come and work for me."

"I seriously doubt that will happen after you double-cross him this way."

"Well, I am going to get a rise out of him, that's for sure. But hell, Charlie would never hurt me. We go way back. Besides, what's it to you? You'll get your hundred and fifty."

Back at the pick-up stop, Charles jumped in his car and sped away. *What am I going to do? I can't go back to Don's alone. They would be expecting me, and I wouldn't win this fight.* Don was always heavily armed, and Charles knew that he couldn't sneak up on the pair of them because of the dogs. There was only one option. He would have to go back to Oklahoma City and get "Mad Dog" Magee. Don would regret ever double crossing him. Mad Dog was the muscle whenever there was an issue for the bootleggers. He was a scary-looking man, six-foot-four, blond, with ice blue eyes. He had a long scar running down his left cheek. He would have to swear Mad Dog to secrecy over this matter. If he told Chaney what had happened, he'd have Don killed or beaten to within an inch of his life. There was no mercy for bootleggers who held up other runners. They were hunted down and made examples of, to remind the others what happened to those who robbed the king pins.

But what happened to Don was the least of Charles's worries. What about him? As he raced back to Oklahoma City, he anguished over the fate that awaited him if Chaney found out. He could lose his job, and that was not an option. He didn't want him dead; they went too far back.

During the long drive back, Charles thought back to when it had all started. It was 1955 and he was twenty, working at the parking garage of the Hukins Hotel in Oklahoma City. His job had been to help the runners who brought in their cars loaded down with the liquor. The large parking garage was the perfect setup for Chaney's business. When Chaney came in, Charles would make sure that he noticed him. He'd unload and box up the orders quickly and accurately. He would be extremely polite to Chaney. He made sure he looked neat and tidy and acted like a gentleman, the sort who could handle any situation. This is how Chaney liked his runners to be, and Charles knew it.

Just to make sure he got Chaney's attention, Charles also made an effort to let it be known that he had a knack for speed and was racing cars and motorcycles at the speedway. Chaney did take notice and told Charles that once he turned twenty-one, he would hire him to be a runner. The day finally came.

"I turned twenty-one today," he said, "and I'm ready to go to work for you."

Chaney gave his address to Charles and told him to come over that evening at eight o'clock. When he pulled up to the address, it was a large two-story mansion with a large iron gate. Out of nowhere, a huge man rapped hard on the window.

"Charles Parrott?"

"Yes. I'm here to see Mr. Chaney"

"Go on up, and park by the front door."

Chaney opened the door and took Charles to his office. No offer of a drink or small talk. This was all business.

"I see you have a car, but it won't do," Mr. Chaney told him.

"Yes, sir, well I could trade it for something better."

"I'll set you up with a car. You know. It has to be specialized for the runs. You'll pay me fifty dollars a week until it's paid for. You're gonna wear a suit, boots, and have a pistol. After you're trained, I'll pay you one hundred and fifty a load, and I'll pay the gas and your lunch or dinner. If you get arrested, you take the fall, and you never name anyone. Only you. Odds are it will happen, so you just sit tight. I will give you a phone number to call if you get picked up. My employee, Sally, will come bail you out. You'll say she's your girlfriend. Not a hard thing to admit. She's a doll. Very easy on the eyes. She'll always come for you. If you have to spend some time in jail, that is what will happen, and you'll stay quiet."

Chaney paused, looking closely at Charles. "Are you sure you want to do this? It's dangerous, and you have to think fast on your feet. If someone tries to rob you, you will be in a bad situation."

"I understand. I can handle myself."

Chaney continued, "Could you kill a man if you had to?"

"Yes, sir. If I had to, I would."

"You and your wife cannot tell people what you do for a living. You're married, aren't you?"

"Yes, sir."

"Is your wife a gossip?"

"No, sir. Reba Sue hates gossip and never likes anyone in being nosey about our business. She doesn't even like the neighbors paying us a visit."

"Good to hear. If you have a big mouth, you will be robbed. It's just a known fact. So, can you both keep your mouths shut?"

"Yes, sir."

"Does your wife drink?"

"No, sir. I met her when I was fifteen. She has never taken a drink in all the time I've known her. She is a respectable woman, a good girl all her life from a good family. She has a job working for the State Health Department. You won't have to worry about her."

Chaney grinned and said, "I like her already. Now you know the dangers, so I want you to go home and talk to your wife before you accept the job. She must be on board. I'm not going to train you, put my time and effort into shaping you up, only to have you go and quit on me in a couple of months because your wife just found out what you do for a living. If she agrees and you think you have the guts to do this kind of work, then you're hired. I think you could be good at this.

Charles went home and talked to Reba Sue. She agreed only because she knew he would do it whether she approved or not. The money was good, and they had a young son and another baby on the way. This was part of his ploy to urge her agree. He knew that she loved him, and she would put up with a lot to keep him by her side. That was a couple of years ago, and she was still putting up with him.

As he pulled into his driveway at home, he knew he would have to make a call to Luke, Chaney's second in command, to explain why he didn't bring the liquor in. He told him that he'd left the money for his run at his house and that he would make the run tomorrow. His wife, Reba Sue got out of bed. She overheard his conversation, and as soon as he hung up, she questioned him. He told her the truth.

"Good old Don. How many times has he taken advantage of your friendship? I can't stand him. He even tried to get me to go out with him when you were away our senior year. I hope you never speak to him again."

Charles looked at his wife and thought about how beautiful and feisty she was. Standing only five two with long strawberry blonde hair and those brilliant light green eyes. Of course, Don had tried to make a move on her. Many young men in McCurtain County had a crush Reba Sue Snow. She was the star of the basketball team and played piano at the Baptist Church. She was a good girl with a spitfire attitude.

"He planned it, that's for sure. I'm going right back up there tonight with Mad Dog, and I am going to get my money back!"

Reba Sue was scared. "If you're taking Mad Dog Magee things could get bad real fast. I'm going with you."

"No, you can't go."

"Well, what if I take the kids to see your parents? You will only be an hour away from their home. We've been planning a trip to see them anyway. I'll drive separate, and as soon as you get the money and the load, I'll follow you home. I want to be close by if anything happens to you."

Charles gave in, "Okay, but we have to leave right away."

Reba Sue started packing up the kids while Charles got on the phone with Mad Dog Magee, telling him it was an emergency and to come over as soon as he could.

"And don't tell a soul. This here is a secret mission. I'll pay you on the side."

The plan was set. Reba Sue would drive a couple of hours, then get a hotel for her and the kids. It was a four-hour trip.

She would call her mother-in-law, Odessia, in the morning and let her know that they were on their way. Charles would call her from Pineville as soon as they got the money and let her know how things were going.

Charles and Mad Dog drove through the late night and early morning hours to get there at sunrise. Charles parked the car on a dirt road that ran behind the cabin, they headed out on foot. The plan was simple: they would ambush Don and Melvin.

"Hey, he has some dogs" whispered Charles as he clambered up the ridge just above the cabin."

"Damn it, Charlie, I love dogs. I better not have to shoot one. I don't have any problem shooting a man, but I don't like shooting animals," he whispered back.

The sun was just rising when they approached the cabin. They got about forty yards from the door when one of the dogs became aware of them. First a low growl and then it charged toward them, snarling and barking. Charles fired his gun; it dropped and did not move. The door to the cabin opened and out charged the other one. This time Mad Dog shot first, wounding the dog. It was yelping and going crazy. Gunfire blasted out of an open window of the cabin, and more shots rang out from one of the outbuildings to the west. Bullets were flying as the pair flung themselves behind a big rock.

"How many men does he have here?" asked Mad Dog.

"I think only him and Melvin."

Mad Dog said, "We need a better spot. I think if we split up, we'd have a better advantage."

"Okay, you go to that boulder over there, and I'll stay here. Let me fire off a round and cover you."

As Charles pulled his gun up to aim toward the cabin the sound of a machine gun and a spray of bullets hit the ground and the large boulder they were using for cover.

"Damn it, Charlie, we're not going to win this fight. We gotta get out of here."

They belly-crawled out, staying as low to the ground as they could. Once they were a distance from the cabin, they lay there for a while, breathing hard and cussing.

"I'm sorry. That didn't go as well as I'd expected. I knew they would be waiting for me to come back. I feel stupid for not thinking this through."

Mad Dog said, "We can sit em' out. They can't stay holed up there forever."

"Honestly Dog I'm so damn tired. I just want to get the hell out of here. I am scratched up and eaten up with ticks and chiggers."

"Let's go."

They climbed in the car and drove to a cemetery just south of Pineville. Charles pulled the car under the shade of a large oak tree. Exhausted, they slept in the car for a couple of hours.

Mad Dog woke up and said, "I'm starving to death. Let's go into town and get some food."

"I need something for these bug bites. I think I got into some poison ivy. Dog, we need to get outta these clothes."

They drove into the town of Pineville and bought some sandwich meat and bread. Sitting in the car at the town square, Mad Dog pointed toward the McDonald County Bank.

Mad Dog said, "I believe it would be easier to rob that bank than to try to get the money back from Don."

Charles grinned. "Okay. Let's do it."

The seed had been planted. They started planning the robbery.

Charles and his 1949 Nash

BECOMING A
BANK ROBBER

May 1, 1958, Charles found a payphone and called Reba Sue to tell her what had happened.

"I hate that man," she fumed. "I wish you'd never gone to see him. He's always been trouble for you."

"So, what are you going to do now?" she asked.

"Well, we are going to rob the Pineville Bank. I have a plan. I need you and the kids to meet me at the Pineville cemetery in three hours. Do me a favor and grab those Halloween masks of Tonto and the Green Hornet that I saw Charles Lee playing with at Momma's house last time we were there."

"Charles, you can't be serious."

"Just do what I tell you to do, or don't do it at all and take the kids back to Oklahoma City."

"I'll be there."

"Good, because I need you. The cemetery is on the south side of the town off the main highway. You'll see the sign. I love you, Reba Sue." He hung up before she could say another word.

They drove around the outskirts of Pineville and found the perfect spot to change cars: an old vacant homestead that sat off the main road. They sat there and continued planning the robbery. They would drive into Bentonville, steal a car, and hide their car nearby. Then, they would drive the stolen car to the cemetery to meet Reba Sue. They would lead her to the vacant homestead outside Pineville, where she would wait for them so that once it was all over, they could jump in with her. There were only two highways that led out of Pineville, and so it was important to prepare for a roadblock.

Reba Sue was at the cemetery when the men arrived. She jumped out of the car, leaving seven-month-old Susan and two-year-old Charles Lee sitting in the front seat.

"So, this is family time for us?" she said, smirking at Charles in disbelief. "What the heck are we doing?"

"We're getting ready to rob a bank, baby. Now let's get going."

Reba Sue couldn't help herself. She needed a thrill. This was insane, but she was in it and there was no turning back. They climbed into her 1955 Chevy and headed down Big Sugar Road.

"I brought the masks. One of you will be Tonto and one of you will be the Green Hornet. And here are some pillowcases for the money."

"My smart wife," said Charles, "I'm glad you thought of that."

"Well, there better be a lot of money, not just a handful. And don't shoot anybody or get shot! Just get the money and get out as fast as you can," said Reba Sue.

Charles had instructed her to hide her car down the lane behind the old barn. It was far enough away from the turn in case they were followed.

He gave her the directions to his car at an old, abandoned barn outside of Bentonville. That is where she would drive with them hiding in the trunk.

"Don't speed and just stay calm. No one will suspect a mother and her children. We will be back in less than thirty minutes." He pulled her to him, kissed her, and left.

The children were asleep in the front seat beside her. She watched the men pull away and said a short prayer. After four years of marriage to Charles she had changed. She wasn't sure who she was anymore.

Charles revved up the engine and shot out onto the dirt road. The energy inside the car was intense. Mad Dog was wringing his hands and popping his knuckles. Charles wondered if he'd done something like this before, but he didn't ask him.

Charles said, "When we get inside, I'll stand guard over the people, while you get the money. I'll take the sawed-off shotgun, and you'll carry the .45."

"All right by me," said Mad Dog.

They both took a deep breath.

Charles pulled up right in front of the bank and looked at Mad Dog and said, "What do you think the good Lord would say about us?"

"That we need to get in there and wail."

Then Mad Dog pulled on the mask and out of the car he went, pistol and pillowcases in hand. Charles pulled the mask down and took quick, long strides to catch up with the swift moving giant. Two men were painting up on a scaffold across the street. Charles noticed them, but he didn't slow down, and he didn't look back.

A woman with her two children in the car had just pulled up to the general store. Her son saw the two men in masks with guns and said urgently, "Mommy, those men are going to rob the bank."

The mother saw a younger man sitting in a pickup next to them. "Sir, we just saw two men in masks and carrying guns, going into the bank. I think they are robbing the bank right now."

He had a hunting rifle on the gun rack in the truck and he grabbed it and started toward the bank. Suddenly, he turned around and put the gun back in the truck.

"What are you doing?" the woman asked.

"Ma'am I don't want to die today, and I don't want to shoot anyone."

The woman ran and told the grocery store owner what was happening. The young butcher in the shop called out that he had a rifle in the back, and he ran to get it. Minutes passed, and the shopkeeper went in the back of the store to see the young butcher struggling to load the gun. His hands were shaking badly.

Mad Dog entered the bank with Charles right behind him. There were four people in the bank, two tellers, a lady who was sitting at a desk close to the door, and a man in a small office just off to the right.

"This is a hold up! Everyone down on the floor, now!" Charles hollered.

One of the ladies behind the teller's booth chuckled like it was a joke and didn't move to get down on the floor. The lady sitting at the desk looked at Charles questioningly, unsure if he was joking. He took her by the shoulder and shouted again, "Get down on the floor. Do it now!"

He forced her to the floor as Mad Dog moved around behind the counter and yelled,

"He means it! Now get down!"

Mad Dog hit the teller across the back of her head, and as he did so, the gun went off in his hand. The woman slumped face-down on the floor, unconscious. The shot was deafening. The bullet penetrated the wall, and a woman began screaming. Charles leapt toward Mad Dog, ready to kick his ass for such a stupid stunt. Before he could reach him, another woman appeared from behind the vault door, and Mad Dog hit her with the butt of his gun and she fell down to the floor. *Damn, this is not going well,* Charles was keeping watch as his accomplice went down one side and then the other stuffing bills into the pillowcases. Charles hoped no one else had heard the shot, but then a man came around the corner and looked inside the bank window. Charles went outside and dragged him in. Another lady came up suddenly.

"Get that girl off the street!" Mad Dog hollered, so Charles grabbed her, too.

Charles yelled, "We are leaving now!

"But the vault?" said Mad Dog.

"Leave it. We've drawn too much attention," said Charles.

They raced out of the bank, masks still on and guns raised in case anyone got in their way. They jumped into the stolen Buick and sped away from the curb. Charles saw in the rearview, a young man running toward the bank with a rifle in his hand, while another ran out of the bank to meet him. The pair jumped into a 1955 Ford and were coming after them at top speed.

"Damn it! We got a tail, and they have a rifle," said Charles.

Mad Dog turned and saw the Ford coming as they swung onto Big Sugar Road.

"Dust 'em out," said Mad Dog.

Their Buick was fast, and they were leaving the chase car behind in a cloud of dust. They had gone about four miles down Big Sugar Road and had a mile to go, where Reba Sue was waiting. There were two curves that would hide their turn into the grassy lane of the abandoned house. Hopefully, the chase car would keep going down the road. Charles jumped out of the car and ran to a spot to watch for the chase car. It kept going, and he could see that they turned to the left at the three-way stop sign, just fifty yards away. This was good. They could take the fastest route out to Bentonville as planned.

Charles ran the Buick down into a ravine, hoping it would drop all the way into the canyon below. But there were some trees that prevented its descent, and the car was still visible and running below them. The tires were spinning, and Charles began to move toward the edge to head down and turn the car off.

"Leave the car!" Reba Sue yelled, opening the trunk.

Mad Dog climbed inside, and his giant body took up most of the trunk space.

"I hope there's room for you," said Reba Sue, shaking her head as Charles squeezed into Mad Dog's spoon.

"If I hit the brakes a few times, you'll know there's a roadblock, so have your guns drawn and ready," she said, shutting the trunk.

There were only two ways out of Pineville, and she would be lucky to get past the point where there would be more dirt roads to take. Sure enough, after two miles on Highway 71, she saw the roadblock. There were two police cars, one on each side of the road. As she approached, she tapped the brakes.

"Get that pistol ready," said Mad Dog. "And remember we got five shots since I fired that one in the bank."

"Yeah, I remember."

"Shut up. We're stopping."

One officer jumped into a patrol car and hit the sirens, screeching past her as she was rolling to a stop.

The siren made Mad Dog almost come through the roof of the trunk. Charles could feel his heart pounding against his back. Mad Dog made a low groan and sucked in his breath.

"Quiet, Dog," whispered Charles.

Reba Sue pulled up to the patrolman, and he looked inside, taking in the kids in the front seat. The little baby in a basket and the boy holding a stuffed bear grinning at him. Looking back at Reba Sue, he asked her if she had seen anyone speeding on the highway. Breathing calmly and slowly, she replied that she hadn't, even venturing to ask what had happened.

"We just got a call that two men robbed the Pineville Bank."

"Oh, my goodness!" she gasped. "Is it safe to be on the highway right now?"

"As long as you don't stop for any strangers," he said and walked toward the back of her car. Another cop was on the radio in the police car.

"Marcus, we got to go," the other patrolman called to him. "Davis just radioed in that they have the car that the robbers were driving. They wrecked it, and he thinks he found their tracks going toward Cook's store."

The officer ran to the patrol car, and they sped off in the direction Reba had come from. She let out a long breath and pulled away. Her heart was pounding in her chest like a sledgehammer.

"Thank you, Jesus," she whispered and looked at her kids. Little red-headed Charles Lee was grinning from ear-to-ear, and Susan let out a long yawn.

Charles let out a long sigh. "We made it through. If they had opened the trunk, someone was going to die."

"Yeah, that could have been me. I thought I was having a heart attack when that siren went off. I had bad pain in my chest," said Mad Dog. "I gotta get out of this trunk soon. I feel like I can't breathe."

"Just hold on we don't have far to go. Can you do that, Dog?"

"Yeah," he groaned.

Reba Sue stayed on Highway 71, crossing the state line, and twenty minutes later she pulled up beside the barn where

Charles's car was hidden. She unlocked the trunk and Charles jumped out, grabbing her and swinging her around.

"We did it! We robbed a bank!" yelled Charles. "And it sure wasn't pretty. It was a mess. Mad Dog's gun went off when he struck this poor bank teller that wouldn't do as she was told and then another poor lady came out of the back and he struck her, and she went down."

Reba Sue's eyes got wide, and she did not want to hear that, but then Charles opened the bag and poured the money out onto the floor of the barn. They starting to count their loot. They had six thousand five hundred dollars. Not as much as they had hoped for, but it was enough for Charles to pay Chaney for the lost money. He and Mad Dog had agreed that they would split what was left after Chaney's money, the two thousand, was recovered. They would split the rest.

"What about the get-away driver?" said Mad Dog.

"Well, if you like we can give her a cut."

"She did a damn good job driving and the kids were brilliant."

"Are we paying the kids too?" Charles chuckled.

"Well, probably best we leave them out of this." He counted out a five hundred and gave it to Reba Sue.

"Stay real cool on the road home, and keep this to yourself," he told Mad Dog. "And don't go spending this money right away. Word is gonna spread if Don goes bragging about the double-cross. People will put two and two together. Understand?"

"Yeah, I gotcha."

"When I get back to Oklahoma City, you and I will go to Mexico for the car race like we already planned. We can spend some money down there, and no one will know," said Charles.

"Sounds good. I'll drop the car at your place and see you back in the city. Unless you're going back to Pineville to pick up your load of whisky," said Mad Dog.

"I don't think that would be a good idea. In fact, I may just return this money to Chaney and tell him I am done, and I have a new profession." Charles laughed.

Charles

Reba Sue with their son Charles Lee

GOODBYE BIG CITY

When Reba Sue and Charles got back to Stilwell after the bank robbery, they could hardly contain themselves. They sat on the porch with Charles's mother, Odessia. She was a force to be reckoned with. Odessia always spoke what was on her mind and she didn't care if it hurt anyone's feeling. She was a bit dowdy, with brown hair and those same hazel eyes as her son. And although she was far from fashionable, she was married to the most stylish man in Adair County, Bud Parrott. He was always wearing, an expensive cowboy hat, cowboy shirt, tie, vest, and a big belt buckle, won at some ancient rodeo in his youth. He was the director of the welfare department and everyone in town knew him.

They visited for about an hour chatting about all the mundane goings on in the small town of Stilwell. It was hard for them to control their emotions and keep their minds on the topics of discussion. They kept looking at one another with sly grins and raised eyebrows.

"Mama, could you watch the kids while we take a walk? I wanna show Reba Sue those caves and overhangs where I found those arrowheads. I'm going to take a shovel and dig around. Maybe we'll find some more buried up there."

"Of course, go on and show her."

The pair walked to the back of the house where the car was. Charles climbed inside, pulling several bundles of money from out of the bag. He had taken a large glass jar from his mother's kitchen, and he began rolling bills and stuffing them inside it.

"What are you doing, honey?" asked Reba Sue.

"We are going to hide our nest egg in this jar."

He put the money bag back and they started walking behind the house up to the mountainside. They walked for several minutes with Charles telling her everything about the bank robbery. He stopped suddenly and pointed to a tree with a big rock right next to it.

"There's the perfect spot."

He started digging a hole beside the rock and slid the jar into it.

"This is where our nest egg will be. As soon as we get home, honey, I want you to start packing. We're moving here to Stilwell. I know you hate living in the city, and with my mother and Aunt Polly living here you could have help with the kids."

"I do hate living in the city. I've never felt that we belonged there. I know you liked racing cars and motorcycles, but you didn't get to do rodeo anymore. This could be a good change for us."

"As soon as we return, I'm going to go pay Mr. Chaney, and I want us to come here and find a house. I want to move quickly. I don't want any problems with Chaney about Don DeLow. I'll do right by him, and I'll let him know I'm getting out of the bootlegging business. I just hope Don doesn't go bragging about robbing me. It'll be embarrassing most of all."

"I understand. I'll give notice at work and start packing."

They sat against the big rock by the tree like a pair of teenagers. They were only twenty-two years old. The excitement of what they had done was like a drug. They couldn't be happier. They'd just gotten away with robbing a bank.

"You can't ever tell the kids about what we did," said Reba. "I still can't believe that I have done this."

Charles laughed. "Or that they were with us when we did it. I have corrupted you!"

He thought about how innocent she was when he met her and how innocent she still had been until today.

When they got back to the house, Bud had arrived and was sitting at the dining room table drinking his tenth cup of coffee for the day and chain-smoking cigarettes. Apart from Odessia, nobody knew who Charles's real father was. Everyone would have thought that Bud was his father, except Charles never called him father or daddy. He called him Bud. And that was Bud's preference for some reason. People thought that was peculiar and often asked questions and probed Odessia for answers. But they never got any. She always replied in the same blunt and honest manner. That it was no one's business. Bud had adopted him when he was three years old after marrying her. All of Charles life he wanted to know who his real father was. Odessia was an intimidating woman, and no one wanted to ever battle with her about anything. She loved Charles, but she couldn't bear to tell him that him that his father was a criminal she'd met while working as a nurse close to the prison. She had married him when he was paroled but left him when Charles was a baby and never wanted to see him again.

Aunt Polly, Bud's younger sister, came in the door, and the room filled with the smell of expensive perfume. She always stood out with her designer clothes and lots of sparkling jewelry. Charles Lee toddled into her arms, and she kissed his chubby cheeks. Then she scooped up baby Susan and exclaimed she had bought all the prettiest little baby girl dresses that Catron's shop had. She slipped a gold baby bracelet onto Susan's tiny arm and kissed her head, holding the baby close.

Polly owned the jewelry store in town and was considered high society in Stilwell. She had never married and lived with her mother, Minnie, who everyone called Mom Parrott. They owned a lovely big home outside of town on forty acres. It sat up on a hill and was white frame with white stone. People called it the White House of Adair County. Polly lived a life filled with travel and adventures. There weren't many women business owners in her day, and she did whatever she pleased and was happy for it. Some people in Stilwell thought that Charles was Polly's love child, but he wasn't. You could see those same gold flecked eyes and the slight gap in his front teeth and know he belonged to Odessia.

"I'm so happy you're here. I miss the babies," said Polly.

"Well then, you're going to be happy to hear this news. Reba Sue and I have decided to move to Stilwell. The city life just isn't as good as we thought it would be, and Stilwell would be a good place to raise the kids. What do ya'll think about that?" Charles asked.

Polly jumped up and hugged Charles, telling him it was the best decision he had ever made, and she would help them find a home. Bud offered to get Reba Sue a job at the courthouse.

"Charles, what will you do when you move here?" asked Aunt Polly.

"I've got some ideas, and I'm going to go back to rodeoing," said Charles.

"Oh, honey, please don't go back to riding those bulls again. Could you please change to roping like Bud?" Polly asked.

"Aunt Polly, you know I love that thrill of riding and roping is boring. The guys that ride bulls are my kind of people."

"Are you saying I'm boring?" asked Bud.

"No, Bud, I'm just saying it's boring to me to rope from a horse at a rodeo. I like roping cows when I'm out rounding up strays, but doing it in an arena doesn't appeal to me. You're far from boring."

Odessia chimed in, "I know exactly what Charles is saying. Bull riders are crazy and wild, especially after the rodeo is over. Don't you think it's time to grow up and be a good husband and father to the kids?"

"Mama, I'm a good husband and a good father. I think I'm proving that by moving here," Charles responded.

"He's going to raise cattle and be a cattleman like Bud and my daddy," said Reba Sue. "It's going to be wonderful moving here. We're really excited about it."

Reba Sue wondered what it would be like living here. Odessia was probably going to be a challenge as her mother-in-law. Aunt Polly would be her ally here. She was sure of that since Polly had pulled her aside and told her so.

1958-Polly Parrott with Susan and Charles Lee

Bud and Odessia Parrott

VIAN, OKLAHOMA

SEPTEMBER 26, 1958

Charles was impatient to get back to the country town life and his new career as a bank robber. There had never been a more intense feeling than the one he had experienced upon stepping into the Pineville Bank, and it had only intensified with the chaos that ensued. But the last heist had been risky, and Charles knew that he had to get Mad Dog to settle down a little if he was to be his partner. He decided that he would have him fetching the money while he watched the people inside the bank. Mad Dog had no patience, and his temperament was the sort that would get someone killed.

Polly found Charles and Reba Sue the perfect house, a two-bedroom brick home with a small kitchen and a cozy living room with a large fireplace. It had a barn and forty acres, half of which was pastureland and the other half mountainside. There was a creek that ran through the property that would provide water for the cows and horses. It was perfect, and Reba Sue was thrilled. Her life in Oklahoma City had not been wonderful, and she had tried to like it there, but small-town living is what she yearned for and even though she wished they had moved back to McCurtain County where they first met and where her family lived.

When it came time to leave the city, Charles was acutely aware that he was really going to miss his friends, especially the guys at the racetrack. Just a couple of months ago he had won the Grand Nationals in Dodge City. He had the fastest motorcycle in the nation, a Triumph that he had customized to race. He had a lot of friends in the city, and he could always come back to visit. He knew this was the right move.

After they moved, Charles bought twenty head of cattle. Honey Snow, Reba Sue's father gifted them twenty of his finest cattle. To Charles, this was as an indication that the Snows were finally accepting him as a son-in-law.

Reba Sue got a job working at the welfare department downtown on the square, where they quickly realized that she was the fastest typist they had ever seen. Her fingers would fly over the keys, and she made an all-time record at the office by running through three cylinders of ink in one day.

But despite their earnings, the young couple had used up their nest egg, and Charles realized that it was high time to rob another bank. He and Reba Sue would sit in bed at night reading true crime magazines realizing they needed to plan this next one out down to every detail. This was serious business, and they were keen to learn the tricks of the trade. The planning stage had begun. Together they decided that the next bank should be Vian, Oklahoma, as the town had several back roads that made for speedy access to and from the bank. They could be home in Stilwell before anyone even noticed they had left. They also planned their alibis and were content to find that after careful consideration, they had before them a solid plan.

They'd hire workers to put up a fence line around the property. At a specific hour, Charles would go out there and check on the progress. Then he would casually inform the man that he was going back to the house to spend some quality time with his wife while the kids were out at Aunt Polly's house. Reba Sue would have already called in sick that day, and the two of them would turn up the radio in the house and sneak out the back to a car they had hidden in a lane that ran beside their property. With the worker thinking that the pair of them were laid up in the house and they would be off to Vian. It was the perfect alibi. The worker would be there all day. Reba Sue and Charles would meet Mad Dog at Polly's barn while Polly was in town at work. From there, they would head off to the bank.

Once at Polly's barn, the three of them sat down to go over the plan one last time. Reba and Charles had already cased the bank and filled Mad Dog in on what they had learned. They had observed that one of the bank employees drove a new Ford Coupe, which looked fast. This would be their getaway car. They were due to arrive there around ten thirty, as there weren't usually many customers going in at that time, which meant fewer people to deal with. Instead of the masks worn in Pineville, this time they had decided to wear bandanas like old west outlaws, along with dark sunglasses and overalls. The aim was to look like a couple of poor guys. After robbing the bank, they would meet Reba Sue at a cemetery just a mile away. There they would change into their suits. Nice clothes, not greasy and dirty overalls. That way they wouldn't have to hide in the trunk. They'd be able to ride in the car with her and not look suspicious. Then it would just be a short three miles until they hit the dirt roads back toward Stilwell.

"Sounds good," said Mad Dog.

"Just don't be shooting your gun this time, Dog."

"I'll try."

Dressed like a couple of poor workmen, the two men rode toward the bank with Reba in the driver's seat.

"This time we have to get them all down on the floor right away. Take control immediately," said Charles. "And let me do the talking. I'm going to use a deep Southern accent to throw them off."

"And I'm going to go straight to the vault," said Mad Dog.

"Yeah, that's where the big money is," said Charles.

"Well, we're learning," said Mad Dog.

"And never pull that mask off until we are in the clear. When we get to town we will duck down in the seats. No one sees us get out of the car without our masks already on." Charles didn't want any mistakes this time.

"Get down," Reba whispered. "We are coming into to town."

She pulled around the side of the bank, looking quickly around to make sure no one would see the men get out of her car. Confident that the coast was clear, she gave them the heads up to go.

Charles was nervous. It had not been a good idea to have her drop them off. It made him anxious having her this close to trouble. But here she was, and it was too late to change the plan. So out he jumped, with his heart pounding. He watched as Reba Sue pulled away slowly, heading north up the road toward the meeting spot at the cemetery.

He relaxed a little. They knew what they were doing, and Reba Sue was heading away from danger. She and Charles had spent weeks planning the getaway and had timed the heist to coincide with how long it would take officers from the county seat to get there. They didn't think there was any constable in the town. After the Pineville robbery, they'd decided to never rob a bank that had a police station in the town, only small-town banks where officers would have to travel to get there.

The minute they entered the bank, Charles was in control. He had practiced what he would say. He was calm. It was like he became someone else. He was an actor with a role to play, and he knew just how to do it. His voice was steady, and his accent was good. He was clear and commanding as he announced their presence.

"This is a bank robbery! Everyone down on the floor."

Everyone did as they were told. This time there was no laughter, and no confusion. Charles asked who drove the Chevy Coupe and demanded the keys. A young man raised his hand and slowly took the keys from his pocket.

"That's my brand-new car. You really should take Elle's car. I'm almost out of gas."

"Sorry, but I need it," said Charles.

Charles wasn't fooled by the low gas story, knowing that the man was just saying it so that his car wouldn't be stolen.

"How long will it take you to get that vault open?" he said to the man, while pocketing the keys.

"Not long."

Charles tossed the bag to Mad Dog, who followed the man to the vault. Entering it, he promptly loaded the sack with the largest bills. Then he cleaned out the teller's cash drawers. Nodding to Charles that he was done, the two quickly exited the building. They were in and out in less than five minutes.

They looked out the bank window, making sure no one was outside the bank, walked out the door acting inconspicuous and climbed into the Chevy Coupe. Charles turned the key, and it sputtered. The man hadn't been lying about the gas! The car wouldn't start. Panicking, he looked up and saw a man sitting in a car a few parking spots down from them. He was busy reading the paper, so he didn't notice when Charles walked over and yanked the driver's side door open.

"Get out!"

The man looked at him in disbelief, and then with horror at the sawed-off shotgun pointed directly at him. He jumped out of the car, and Charles and Mad Dog climbed in and started the ignition. It was a 1943 Nash, an old car, and Charles prayed that it would get them to where they needed to meet Reba.

A bank teller called the police and told them what kind of vehicle the bank robbers were driving. The highway patrol were alerted, and they alerted patrolmen to throw up road-blocks on Highway 64 east of Vian. They also employed spotter planes to try to spot the car.

Charles was mad. He guided the old Nash down the road, chugging along at forty miles per hour, as this was the fastest it would go. He saw the look of surprise on Reba's face as he cruised up in the old car.

Jumping out of the vehicle, the two men climbed out of the filthy clothes and put them in a bag, dressing rapidly in the smart suits. Charles was cussing about the car, but Mad Dog was just happy to have a big sack full of money. The Buick that Reba drove had a side panel that they had made loose, and they slid the money bag into the panel. There was so much that they could barely get it inside. Reba drove to the hole they had dug the week before on the side of the road, just a little way from the cemetery, and Charles jumped out, put the clothes and the guns in the hole and covered it with a large rock. Reba Sue pulled out on Highway 64 and made it to the dirt road without seeing any cops. She pulled over and let Charles do the driving back to Stilwell. As Charles spun out pulling onto the dirt road, Mad Dog hooted and laughed in the back seat about how it had been like taking candy from a baby, but suddenly he clutched his chest and groaned.

Reba Sue was a nervous wreck. Maybe they should have hidden the money there with the clothes and guns. No. They couldn't trust Mad Dog. *Sure, he was a good guy,* she thought, *but that was a lot of money, enough to tempt anyone. We are criminals,* she reflected, *and you can't trust criminals.*

They pulled into Polly's barn, where Mad Dog had left his car. Vian was a very small-town bank, but they had taken an incredible haul. They counted a little over sixteen thousand dollars, they split the figure and gave Mad Dog his share.

"You two are on your own from here on out. You don't need me around. I'm way too jumpy for this kind of work," said Mad Dog.

He told them that his split was enough to head to California, buy a home, and find a beautiful wife. He planned to start a marijuana business where he could run the contraband over the Mexican border. He said that he didn't want to push his luck anymore. Marijuana was going to be the big thing with the boys coming back from Vietnam. Bootlegging whisky was on its way out, and he was sure that bank robbery was going to give him a heart attack. Both heists had left him with a tightened chest, and he knew it wasn't going to be good in the long run.

Charles was relieved that Dog wanted out. He knew that it was hard on a man to walk into a bank and not know if he was going to come out of that building alive.

"I love you, Dog. You're a good friend and a good partner. Drive safe and go bury that money till you feel the coast is clear."

THE BULL RIDERS

A month hadn't passed before Charles decided to dip into some of that Vian Bank money. It was October, and he wanted to do some bull riding before the season ended. After all, it had the potential to be an investment. If you had what it took to ride a wild beast for eight seconds, you could win some decent money. Charles and his friend, Chester Dugun, went to the Fort Gibson Rodeo.

Charles had drawn a bull named High Fly, which was known in the rodeo circuit for being a tough ride. He was a mean beast, huge and ugly, a Brahma-Hereford mix, brown with a white circle around one of his eyes. One of his horns was broken and jagged. Nobody ever wanted to draw High Fly, but Charles took it in stride.

Charles always wore a tall crown hat, and the one he had on that day was a deep green. He had stuffed foam padding into the seat of his Wrangler jeans to soften the fall. His signature white pearl-buttoned shirt gleamed in the bright light of the arena. His chaps were a deep brown, and his boots were made of the finest leather, with the spurs polished enough to blind a man. He climbed up on the chute and on to the big beast. Chester pulled the rope around his gloved hand.

"You ready for this one?" Chester asked. "This son of bitch is one nasty bull."

"Honestly, I'm feeling pretty damn good. I hope I feel this good when the ride is over!"

He moved around, positioning himself on the bull's back, cinching his rope just right. With a nod of his head, he indicated that he was ready.

The gate was pulled open, and High Fly tore out of the chute, kicking his back feet into the air and twisting to the right. But Charles sat up on him balancing with each twist and turn. He was having the ride of his life.

The world was spinning out of control, and all he could see was a blur of lights. He could hear the crowd cheer. This was a rush that only a bull rider felt. High Fly was not short on energy, determined to get the rider off his back. But Charles was more determined to stay on. He thought he heard the buzzer, but he wasn't sure. Things had gone into slow motion as they sometimes did when he was having a good ride. Then High Fly threw him into the air, and he landed on his ass.

He walked away toward the gates as the rodeo clown was working the bull. But just as Charles was about twenty feet from safety, High Fly came running fast toward his back. Unaware, Charles was relaxed and walking slowly toward Chester, grinning like the Cheshire Cat. His smile dropped as he noticed the terrified expression on Chester's face. Looking over his shoulder, Charles saw the bull coming and took off like a rocket, jumping on the fence and looking like a scared little boy. The audience gasped and then a big cheer arose from the crowd. Charles felt like he was the king of the world. He had ridden that beast to the buzzer, and that accomplishment drove him high into the sky, only to be brought crashing back down to earth. There was going to be some prize money tonight, and a buckle would come with this win.

That night, he booked two hotel rooms in Fort Gibson. He called Reba Sue and told her about riding High Fly and winning the prize money, and he also broke the news that he would not be coming home that night.

Chester and some of the guys came into the hotel room to drink whisky and smoke some marijuana. Charles offered to buy drinks for all of them at the bar and told them if they wanted to stay the night, he had the extra room. Most of the guys who had brought their horses had to get on home, but some of the bull and bronc riders took him up on it.

He loved the excitement of the rodeo. Tomorrow he would be sore as hell, and he certainly would not have much of the prize money left, but he didn't give a damn. He always lived in the moment and never worried much about the future.

On the drive home the next morning, he and Chester laughed about how High Fly almost got him. Charles's back hurt like hell, so he asked Chester to drive and then popped a couple of painkillers that his friend had given him. He laid his head against the window and fell asleep with the shiny buckle in his hand and a grin on his face.

A week later, Charles and his good friend, Tommy Porter went to a rodeo in Springdale, Arkansas. In the past, Tommy had told Charles that he had aspirations to work in the rodeo business. Before the rodeo began that night, Charles was socializing with the rodeo organizers, and they told him that the announcer that night wasn't going to make it and they were scrambling to find a replacement. Charles saw this as an opportunity for Tommy.

"You boys are lucky. I happen to be here with one of the best announcers in the business. I'll go fetch him for you," said Charles.

Charles hustled down to find to Tommy and took him to his truck.

"Tommy, I got you a job with the rodeo tonight. They need an announcer, and I told them you were one of the best and I would bring you up to announcers stand."

"Charlie, I don't know if I can do it," said Tommy with a worried look.

"You can do it. You got the personality for it. Now let me dress you up a little."

Charles took off his big diamond ring and told Tommy to put it on, then he pulled out a nice jacket he had and gave it to Tommy.

"There now you look like the real deal. Let's go."

"Charles, you think they will buy it?" asked Tommy.

"Heck yeah, you'll be great. This is your chance, and I can't believe that I get to make this happen for you. Now get up there and show em what you got."

Tommy did an outstanding job. His colorful commentary and knowledge of the technique of a rodeo rider proved that Tommy was destined to be a success. Years later, he would develop his own bucking bull stock and produce some of the best bulls in the nation. Tommy became a rodeo icon. And it all started that night, by Charles believing in him.

Charles especially loved rodeo rider, Rosey Harper. Rosey was a good bull rider and sometimes if Charles was apprehensive about riding a bull, Rosey would step in and ride for him. Charles was very superstitious and believed in lucky charms when it came to riding bulls. He would always tuck one pants leg in his boot and carry a rabbit's foot and some salt in his pocket. One night he didn't want to ride a bull he'd drawn. The bull, Old Pet was a real bucker. No one had been able to complete a ride on him. Charles pulled Rosey aside and asked him to ride for him. Rosey had already ridden his drawn bull, and so they went back to Charles's truck, and they traded shirts. Rosey went right back to the chute area.

"Hey, didn't you just ride Yellow Man?" asked the flank man as he was adjusting the flank strap around the bull.

"Nope, that was my brother, Rosey." he answered and winked at the flank man.

The flank man smiled and went about his business.

ON HIS OWN

As the months went by, Charles and Reba Sue planned their next bank heist. Reba brought home more true crime magazines, which were helpful in planning getaways and establishing alibis. She was hooked on reading them and would stay up late into the night reading. She also studied the banks, the towns, and the maps with Charles. They had decided that the next one would be in Westville, a small town that was only fifteen miles from their home. They were planning this one with just the two of them, and so it was going to be a little more difficult. Charles would be on his own.

Reba had gone inside the bank and checked it out, getting change from the teller and having an opportunity to glance around and locate the vault. It was right next to the teller booths so Charles would be able to keep an eye on the teller and have them empty the vault while he watched customers and employees.

Mad Dog was gone, and the thought of robbing the bank alone scared Charles. No backup, just Reba Sue driving getaway.

It was January 23, 1959, and there had been a horrible snowstorm a few days before that had closed the roads, which had only just started to clear a little. Reba tried to get Charles to put off the robbery because of the weather, but he disagreed. They were both good drivers in snow and on ice, and the chance of a roadblock would be lessened because of the weather. Charles viewed the bad weather as a positive, but it made Reba nervous. What if she slid off the road before getting to the switching place?

This time he didn't wear a mask. Instead, he wore dark sunglasses and had grayed his hair and eyebrows, to appear older. He wore his tan cowboy boots and a gray and black checkered trench coat, and he wore a black fedora hat that belonged to his friend, Slim. He knew Slim would be mad that he wore it because it was one of his favorites, but he'd left it in Charles's car the week before, and it looked good with the trench coat. He looked like Dick Tracy.

They headed up north toward Westville. It was only fifteen miles away, but with the snow and ice, it was slow going. Charles paid one of his friends, Rosey Carter, to come out and feed his cows. He told Rosey to wear the clothes he left him in the barn. This would give Rosey the signature Charles Parrott look: wool coat, sunglasses and the dark felt green cowboy hat. This way, at around nine o'clock that morning his neighbors would drive by and see what they would assume to be Charles's feeding his cows at his usual time of the morning. The plan was for Rosey to stay out there until a few of the neighbors had seen him and he was instructed to write down the time and the name of anyone that he saw.

As they drove over to Westville, Charles was nervous about doing this one alone. He decided he would take a car from one of the employees again. He was chain-smoking Lucky Strikes, trying to calm his nerves. As they got close to town he pulled over and let Reba Sue drive.

"These roads are slick. Don't drive fast, Charles, once you're out of there. This is dangerous. I think we should put this off."

"No, we're doing it."

As she pulled around the corner from the bank and said, "Get in there, and get that money."

"See you in a jiffy," he replied.

His nerves were jumping. Suddenly, he, too, thought about calling it off. He went into the small café nearby and purchased some gum. When he walked out, he noticed a man and a woman pulling up in a '51 Dodge. They went into a business nearby, and Charles walked over to the car and saw that the keys had been left in it. This gave him a thrust of confidence. He pulled the hat down over his eyes opened the car door and grabbed the keys. Time to go.

He turned around and headed straight for the bank. Opening the door, he almost ran right into Emma Jean Hankins, one of his neighbors from Stilwell. He lowered his head as she passed him and as soon as she was out the door, he pulled the pistol from his coat. There were five customers inside the bank, a large number for a snowy day.

"This is a holdup, and I mean business! I want you folks to move behind the tellers and stand facing the wall. Do what I ask, and no one will get hurt."

He was so nervous without a mask. He had thought that it wouldn't be a big deal thanks the graying powder in his hair, as well as the sunglasses and hat, but he felt naked.

Suddenly a man appeared from the vault in the back of the bank.

"What is going on here?" The man asked.

"This is a holdup. If you touch any buttons to alert the police, I'll blow your head off. Now get the money out of the vault for me."

Charles realized with horror that he had left his money bag in the car. He could hardly breathe. The man handed him a stack of bills from the vault, but he had nowhere to put them.

He stuffed the money in the pockets of the trench coat. Things were not going well. He hadn't even asked the tellers for the cash in the drawers. Things were spiraling out of control. A strong wave of nausea hit him, and his stomach hurt. He had to get out of there.

The people were staring at him. Rushing toward the door, he called back to them in a shaky old man voice, "This money will help pay off my farm!"

The couple that owned the car he planned to steal were standing nearby. He jumped in their Dodge but had some trouble starting it, which gave the man time to realize what was happening and approach the car. Charles pointed the pistol at him, and the man backed away. Finally, the car started and off he went. Just as he pulled out of the parking space the man from the bank came out with a rifle, raising it as if to fire at him. Charles slouched in the seat just in case, but he heard no shot. Looking again in the mirror, he saw the man with the rifle get into a truck with another man. They were coming after him and the old Dodge wasn't going to outrun them. He swerved around a corner and then another. His car was slow, but his bootlegging days had trained him to lose someone quick. He made it out of the residential area over to Highway 59. As he was leaving the city limits a cop passed him coming the other way and the cop waved at him in a friendly way. He did not wave back, but instead pressed the old Dodge to go as fast as it would go. It topped out at forty miles per hour.

He made it the two miles to where he passed Reba Sue, who was sitting at a stop sign on a dirt side road. He flashed the lights of the car. It was his signal to her that it was him, and he wasn't being followed. If she'd seen him go by without flashing the lights and he tapped the brake lights, then he was being followed and she wasn't to move. He watched as she pulled out behind him. He was almost to the dirt road where they were to ditch the car when the old Dodge sputtered like it was running out of gas. He panicked and pulled over, leaving the stolen car running and in gear. It went off the road and down into a ravine.

Reba pulled up beside him, and he jumped into the car, his face told the story. Things had gone badly. She hoped he hadn't killed anyone.

As they pulled away, he realized that he had left Slim's hat on the seat, but there was nothing he could do about it. He immediately started taking off the clothes putting everything in the bag that he'd left in Reba's car.

"That car was running out of gas! Thank God, there's no traffic. Hurry, honey, get to that damn road so I can hide the coat, gun, and the money!"

"I can't drive any faster. It's too dangerous."

"I just passed a cop, and there were people chasing me out of the bank with a rifle. This is not going the way we planned."

"Calm down, Charles. We're going to make it."

"I was so nervous. I forgot the bag. Damn it, honey, I barely got any money."

"We're almost there, Charles."

Reba's heart was banging hard in her chest, and her knuckles were white from gripping the steering wheel on the snowy road, and she couldn't stop looking in the rearview mirror to see if someone was going to come bearing down on them. She was scared. The little dirt road was around the next curve. She slowed down and pulled onto the road going slowly to avoid sliding into a ditch. They would be safe once they got to the hiding place. She pulled up to where he had dug the hole and he hopped out and deposited the sack.

He put on his cowboy hat and sunglasses and took over driving back home to Stilwell. His serious look told her not to speak. He couldn't keep his eyes off that rearview mirror.

"Are you okay?" he asked.

"Yeah, I'm okay. Let's just get finished with this, and we'll be fine."

He nodded his head and gave her a smile. He didn't ever want her to do this again. He would find someone else. She could still help, but she couldn't be with him after a robbery.

"Baby, you will not believe it, but I ran into Emma Jean Hankins as I was walking into the bank. I should have listened to you and called it off today. Anything and everything went wrong today."

"Did she recognize you? You didn't kill or shoot anyone, did you?"

"No, she didn't realize it was me. She was walking out as I was coming in. It scared the hell outta me. After that I wasn't composed at all. I don't know what happened. I don't like going in alone. Then I didn't have the bag for the money, I just took a big stack of bills and left. I left a lot of money. I messed this one up."

"It'll be okay. We're almost home," she said, looking over her shoulder.

"I used the shaky voice the whole time and made myself sound like an older man. But I will tell you that will never happen again. I've got to have a mask. I felt exposed and not having anyone to have my back made me feel vulnerable. I need a partner. And when that damn car started sputtering, hell, I wasn't ready for that bullshit. To top it off, I left Slim's hat in that car."

They made it home and could finally breathe. Rosey wasn't in the house, so Charles went to the barn to see if he was there. He found Rosey brushing old Tony, the buckskin horse.

"Did a few folks see you out here this morning?" asked Charles.

"Yup, they sure did. One being Emma Jean Hankins just a little while ago at ten thirty and then Jeb Corey drove by and honked and waved, and I gave him a wave back. That was at ten o'clock."

"Perfect." said Charles. He was feeling good about the alibi.

"Now, Rosey, you don't say a word to anyone. I paid you fifty dollars an hour, and if you prove to me that you can keep your mouth shut, I'll give you another hundred in a month when you've proved that you're solid. You better be good to your word if you want to work for me in the future. Probably the easiest money you'll every make."

Rosey gave him a good firm handshake and swore he'd keep it a secret.

When the newspaper came out that Thursday, Charles couldn't wait to read it. The report on the robbery stated that the police believed the man to be in his late thirties, not the sixty-year-old he was trying to portray. But hell, that would do. Charles was only twenty-five. And now he knew that three thousand five hundred and eighty dollars was sitting in the hidey hole.

After Westville, Charles was certain that he never wanted to rob a bank by himself again. His confidence was shattered. He needed a partner, and he knew it. He decided to call upon his best friend, Slim. He and Slim had bootlegged together and had been friends since they were thirteen, but would Slim be brave enough to do this? He would invite him to Stilwell, and they could talk about it.

SLIM JAMES

S lim came to Stilwell on a Friday night to spend the weekend at Charles and Reba Sue's place. He was living in Tulsa at the time and working for his cousin in the construction business. He wasn't a good-looking man, but a rugged looking one, with wavy blond hair and blue eyes. Women did admire him for his good sense of humor, and he did look like the actor, Steve McQueen.

As he approached the front door, he could hear Charles and Reba Sue fussing.

"Hey, Slim. Thank God you're here," said Reba Sue. "I hope you can talk some sense into Charles. He is up to his crazy, compulsive self again."

She gave Charles a pointed look.

"I'm gonna fix us a late dinner."

"You know how I love your cooking, Reba. What are you fixing?'

"It's a surprise, which means you will have to be here to find out. I know you two will be out howling at the moon since you don't get to see one another as much. So, dinner will be at midnight, and you'll have to be here to find out what's cooking."

"Hey, sweet Reba," Slime crooned, smiling. "What ya got cooking? "

Then Slim grabbed her hand and swung her around to dance. Slim knew the way to make this girl smile. They all chuckled and the mood in the house calmed. Charles motioned for Slim to head on out while he took Reba back into the kitchen. They had gone through these motions a hundred times. Charles could calm that Snow temper most of the time.

Slim went out to his new Pontiac and lit up a pipe filled with marijuana. After a few good tokes, he pulled a half pint of whisky out of the glove box. Slim knew Reba Sue was good for Charles, and he loved her for it. She kept him happy most of the time and gave him pretty the freedom to do his thing. Most women would never put up with his antics. Although that didn't mean that she would take any shit. She could let you have it with both barrels.

Out the door came Charles, walking fast toward the car. He called out to Slim as he approached.

"Fire up that new car and let's get the hell outta here! Quick, while she's on the phone."

Slim fired up the Pontiac and off they went.

"Damn this car is fast!" whooped Charles. "We could do some drag racing in this baby."

"Hell, yeah, we could," Slim replied.

"Remember when we ran liquor for Chaney and raced cars and motorcycles every weekend? I heard that Gary Nixon is sponsored with Triumph and he's winning a lot of races. Sometimes I miss those days."

"Yeah, I miss 'em too," said Slim. "But I also know how you like to be a big fish in a little pond, and I know you love that cowboy shit. I do miss bootlegging. Those were some wild times."

"Heck, we've been best friends ever since we were thirteen. That damn Don Delow introduced us. At least he was good for something. You're the brother I never had. You're the one person I can trust with all my secrets."

"And Lord knows you got secrets," Slim chuckled. "How is the bank robbing business going for ya?"

"Well, it's going really good. I just robbed one over in Westville all by myself." The subject had come up on its own, and so Charles decided to test the water. "Now let me tell ya, I don't like going in a bank alone with no one having my back."

"What happened to Mad Dog? I thought he was your partner."

"Well, Dog was a little to pistol happy. He was scaring me, and I was afraid someone was gonna get shot. Fortunately, he was the one who decided that it wasn't for him."

"Is that right?"

"He said he was afraid he was gonna have a heart attack, so he took his money and headed out to Hollywood, California. Said he was gonna start running marijuana from Old Mexico. Reckons it's going to be the newest and hottest commodity. Heck, he might be right."

"Well, he sure does loves to smoke it," added Slim.

"Slim," Charles started, cautiously, "I wanted to ask you if you would be my new bank robbing partner. I promise you it will be well planned out. Reba and I have been coming up with the best ideas for disguises and getaways. And the pay is good."

"I don't know, Charlie, "said Slim. He took a long pull off the pint of whisky and nodded his head, saying "I'll think it over Charles. I'll let you know in a couple of days."

"Okay Slim. I hope you will. I need you."

"I have to really ponder on this one. We have done a lot of crazy things, but nothing like this."

They headed over to the pool hall. Slim beat a couple of guys out of a few bucks. Charles wasn't much of a pool player, but he loved to bet on Slim when he was playing. And when he won, Charles would buy the loser of the pool game a drink. Charles had a good time everywhere he went and always tried to make sure everyone else was having a little fun too.

When they got back to the house, Reba Sue had cooked up some chicken and biscuits and there was a peach pie in the oven. Slim went to bed with a full stomach and a lot on his mind.

The next morning, Slim woke to the wonderful smell of breakfast. Reba was setting the table when he entered the room with his hair standing straight up on his head.

"Are you going to help us, Slim? We sure do need ya." Reba Sue asked nonchalantly.

"I'm kind of scared to, Reba. You know I don't like violence. Things could go wrong, and someone could get shot. Anything could happen."

"It's crazy and exciting," she teased, with a grin.

"Maybe I could help y'all out this one time," mumbled Slim.

"Well, you could just see how you like it. It isn't for the faint at heart."

"Charles said that Mad Dog felt like he was going to have a heart attack in the middle of a robbery."

Reba looked at Slim and saw the worry on his face.

"Yeah, this robbery business wasn't for him. He is a brute with a fragile heart. He didn't make a good partner. He reacts too strongly. He hurt a couple of women by hitting them with his gun, and Charles didn't like that. He knows that you're levelheaded and loyal, Slim. That's why he wants you. I hope you'll do this with us."

"I'm in. Just for one though to see if I'm cut out for this," Slim said looking up toward the ceiling and shaking his head.

Charles came into the room and slid his arms around Reba Sue.

"Slim's in," she said.

A big grin spread across Charles's face.   "She talk you into it?"

"Yep, you know I can't resist her cooking."

Charles and Slim finished breakfast and they hopped in Charles's truck and headed east to Arkansas to little town called Elkins.

"I tell you, moving back to Stilwell was the best decision I've ever made. Reba Sue would rather be back in Broken Bow, but she is much happier here than she was in Oklahoma City."

"I'm happy for both of you. I know when you left Oklahoma City everyone missed you at Chaney's. He did find out what happened between you and Delow, but he said he didn't hold it against you."

"I knew he would find out. I'm sure Don bragged about it."

"Hell, yeah, he did. I still can't believe he would double cross you like that."

"Well, he just thought he was getting back at Chaney."

"Have you talked to Don since then, Charlie?"

"Yeah. I called him and he said he was sorry. To him it was like a prank. But don't you say nothing about him in front of Reba Sue. She hates his guts."

"Some prank. I could never let him off like that. But you're a different breed, Charles."

"I may forgive him, but I won't forget what happened."

They pulled into Elkins around noon. It was a small town.

"Look at that little bank. That's a cream puff," Charles laughed.

Driving around town, Slim pointed out that there was no police station.

"Yeah, Reba Sue already did that research. The police have to come from Fayetteville," Charles informed him. "That's a twenty-minute drive with no traffic. We will time it so that there won't be many people there during the robbery. Reba Sue and I already drove through there a month ago just to scope everything out. I don't want anyone noticing a stranger lurking around, so I usually take Reba Sue with me because it's better to go as a couple. People are less likely to remember a couple as being out of place. I sent Reba Sue into the bank, and she buys a money order. She scopes it out and sees where the vault is and who might be in charge of the place. Then we wait and let some time go by."

"Sounds like you already have this one figured out."

"Sure do, Slim. We have already cased this one and we want to do it soon. We are working on the disguises now. I just need a partner that I can trust. All you have to do is keep an eye on the door and the people once we get them where we want them. I do all the talking. You would just need you to watch my back Slim."

"After we rob the bank, we'll take a car from one of the employees as our getaway vehicle. Sometimes I like to steal a car, but it's just as easy to take one from someone at the bank."

Slim looked puzzled and asked, "We steal a car from a customer or employee?"

"Yeah, less frontend work. You'll see."

"There are several routes out of Elkins. Let's go driving and scout out our getaway. The planning of the getaway is the most important part."

Charles pulled out on the highway and headed south.

"We gotta go south because the police will be coming from the north."

After about five miles he saw a sign for the Shumate Cemetery.

"Perfect." Charles commented and he swung onto the road that went up a hill. "I love this road. No one could see you up here from the main highway. We have found our spot."

"Have we now?"

"I like using cemeteries. No one bothers you there. This is where we will change clothes and cars. Reba Sue will drop us off at the bank, and then she will drive to this place. Then we will drive out of here with her. We'll leave the stolen car here. Now we gotta find a nearby spot to bury the loot, guns and disguises."

Charles drove back to the highway turned north and went half a mile and turned off on a dirt road, went a little way and stopped. He got out and grabbed the post hole digger out of the back of the truck.

"Gotta have your bank robbing tools," said Charles.

He went across the bar ditch, looked around to make sure no one was in sight and started digging near a fence line. After that he found a rock to put over the hole. He looked around and then went to the truck and got a handkerchief and ripped a strip of cloth from it. He tied it to the barbed wire fence next to hole.

"We will bury everything here."

"Even the money?"

"Yeah. We trust each other, don't we? The one thing I have to make sure of is that we don't get caught after the robbery. And the faster we move out of the area the better chance we have. You and I can lay low together for a couple days and then drive back over and see what we got. It's kind of like a box of Cracker Jacks, and you never know what the prize is till you get to the bottom. Or what I like to do is to listen to the radio or get the newspaper the next day and find out how much money we got."

"Sounds like a solid plan Charlie."

"The FBI will look for us for a couple of days and then leave. At least, that is what they have done in the past. I love reading the newspaper articles after it's over."

Slim grinned and said, "I'm excited about this. When are we going to do it?"

"In two weeks."

March 6, 1959

Slim came into town late Wednesday night from Oklahoma City. On the way, he questioned whether he could really do this. Robbing a bank could end up getting him killed or arrested. But he had faith in Charles. He made it sound like easy money, and he'd successfully robbed three banks already. When Slim pulled up to the house at midnight, the lights were on. Charles came out to greet him.

"Well, Slim are you ready?"

"Ready as I'll ever be. Are you ever ready to rob a bank?"

"You just have to practice what you're going to say. Like an actor practices his lines and then you put on your disguise, and you become a character, you change who you are the minute you walk in the bank door. On the last bank, I dressed like an old man, graying my hair and eyebrows, changing my voice to sound like a shaky old man."

Slim nodded his head and listened intently.

"When we're getting ready, it's like a football player putting on his uniform or a cowboy putting on his spurs. You're getting ready to go in the game. Here's our uniforms for tomorrow."

He tossed two black stocking caps on the dining room table, along with some dirty old clothes like bums would wear.

"These are our tools for the job," said Charles as he laid the two pillowcases and the guns on the table. There was a .38 Special and sawed-off shotgun."

Slim pulled on his stocking cap trying it out. Charles had cut two eye holes so once ready they could pull the caps down and still see. It was March and cold out, so they would not look out of place in the woolen caps.

"Tomorrow, put these on over your clean getaway clothes," Charles instructed. "That way it will be an easy change once we get away from the bank. The most important thing is to stay calm in there. And don't talk much. Especially don't say my name. You will stand guard over the door and make sure that the employees act right. I will have you watch whoever I choose to empty the cash drawers, and I'll take someone in the vault with me. If anyone comes in the door, you will make them lay on the floor."

"And what if they don't act right?" said Slim.

"Oh, they will. Believe me. They will be scared, and so they'll do whatever we tell them to."

It was time for the pair to turn in. Sleep was important because they needed to be alert in the morning. Charles had arranged for Rosey to come over early to get his truck. The plan this time was for him to wear Charles's hat and sunglasses and drive around Stilwell. Anyone who saw him would think that Charles Parrott was out for a drive. He would have a clipboard and had been instructed to write down everyone he saw, so that if Charles needed an alibi, he could call on those people to provide one. Reba Sue was to call in sick so that she could drive them over. She had insisted on being a part of it, even though he didn't want to involve her anymore. He would have to ease her out of the robberies.

Charles handed Slim a blanket and a pillow and headed to the bedroom.

"You got any bank robbing pills to help me sleep?" Slim asked.

Charles chuckled and went and got a sleeping pill for Slim and a glass of water.

The next morning, Slim woke up to the smell of coffee and bacon. His nerves had taken his appetite that morning, but the enticing smells coming from the kitchen changed his mind.

"Good morning, Slim," Reba Sue said. "You like your coffee black, right?"

"Yes, please, and I need it."

"Let me get a good breakfast in you and about four cups of this strong coffee, and you will be fine. Besides, the temperature is twenty-five degrees, and that will sure wake you up."

"Well, we will be wearing two layers of clothes so that's a good thing. I hope I don't mess anything up today."

"Slim, just be quiet once you get inside, and let Charles do all the talking," said Reba seriously. "You know how good he is at talking. And he's good at getting people to do what he wants. So just hold your gun steady and look good. You'll be in and out of there in less than five minutes."

Charles walked in and gave Reba Sue a kiss on her cheek, as she poured another cup of coffee for Slim.

"Slim, I hope you got some sleep."

"Hell, no I didn't. I'm too nervous."

Charles slapped Slim on the back and said, "We are gonna be over there and back within two hours. You'll be surprised how quickly we get this done. Then you'll have a nice pile of money to do whatever you like with. Just relax, Slim, you're gonna be fine."

They ate breakfast and got into their clothes. Charles pulled out the masks, guns, and sacks and they were ready to go.

"When we get close to Elkins, Slim, we'll need to sink down in the seat. Reba will make sure that the coast is clear. Once she does, we get out of the car quick, and you just follow me. Got it?"

"Yeah, I got it. I'll follow you and keep my mouth shut. You'll do all the talking, and when we get out, you'll do the driving, right?"

"Right, and once we're out of the bank and in the car, you take the money and guns, moving them to one of the bags. Then there is another curve and that is where we leave the main road to the cemetery. If the coast is clear, we take the stolen car and run it off the road. I don't want the law catching on to my use of cemeteries."

The sign for Elkins came into sight. Suddenly, everything turned slow motion. The guys slid down in the seat as Reba Sue slowed down. It was time to get serious. Charles grabbed the two pillowcases and tossed one to Slim.

"Now when we get in there, just let me do the talking, Slim."

Slim nodded his head, as Reba Sue pulled up to a stop around the block from the bank.

"There isn't a soul around. Looks pretty good to me. I'll see you guys soon. Good luck," said Reba Sue.

Charles pulled the cap on and looked at Slim, motioning him to do the same. Then out the car they went, taking long, quick strides toward the bank. As soon as they were out of the car, Reba Sue drove away. She didn't like leaving them without a getaway car, but this was how Charles wanted to do it. They would take an employee's car and ditch it down the road.

When Charles and Jim rounded the corner to the bank, there was no car in front of it.

"Damn, there is usually a fifty-four model Ford sitting there. I've cased this four times, and that Ford is always parked out front."

"Ah, someone will come along. What else are we gonna do?" says Slim, and he walks toward the bank.

"I don't know, Slim."

Slim keeps walking and goes on inside the bank door. Charles hurries to catch up with him. As soon as they entered the bank, Charles was in control. With Slim at his side, he felt confident.

"Everybody, this is a holdup! Just do as I say, and no one will get hurt."

This time he was using a Cajun accent. Slim grinned under his mask. Charlie was good at this.

"Sir, I need for you to empty the cash drawers," said Charles.

Charles motioned for Slim to oversee the man and the cash drawers. Slim threw the bag at the employee, and he moved behind the teller's windows. But the man was moving too slowly, and so Slim hit him in the mouth with the butt of the gun.

"You're moving too slow!"

Speeding up, the man rapidly started emptying the drawers into the pillowcase.

"Madame, I need for you to open the vault," Charles said to another of the tellers.

The woman did as she was told and turned the dial on the vault.

"Sir, I can empty all the safe deposit boxes, but the safe inside the vault is on a time lock. It will only open at noon and again at three in the afternoon."

"Then, empty those boxes."

Once the boxes were emptied, Charles instructed the three employees to enter vault, and he and Slim sat there waiting for a customer to show up with a car. Slim was sweating in the double layer of clothes and cussing that this getaway plan was not a good idea. After about fifteen minutes went by a customer came in.

Acting quickly, Charles spun round and pointed his gun at the customer.

"You got a car, mister?"

"Yes, sir, right outside. The green Chevy."

"Give me the keys and get in the vault," he commanded. Now don't come out of there for at least ten minutes."

The pair dashed out the door with the masks still on. Furtively looking around to make sure they were alone. They were relieved to find that there was still not a soul on the streets. Charles jumped behind the wheel and peeled out of the parking space onto the highway, then headed south. Slim started stuffing the guns into the bag with money, all the while looking over his shoulder.

"There isn't anyone following us, Charlie. I reckon we could slow down some."

"To hell with that kind of thinking, Slim. If there's one thing that is of utmost importance, it is getting away quickly. We got a few more miles before we reach the cemetery. Once we get there, I'll be much more comfortable."

"Damn that time lock," said Slim.

"I know, but we are going back in a couple of months and I'm gonna time it so that we get into that safe. The girl told me when it opens, and I doubt they think that we'll be back," he chuckled.

"Shit, Charles, you can't rob the same bank twice!"

"Why not?"

"Well, they might be better prepared for a robbery now."

"Doubt it, and that little bank was nice and easy. Except for the part where you busted that fella in the mouth."

"Well, he wasn't moving fast enough, and you said we gotta be in and out in less than five to ten minutes. So, I had to make him move."

"Let's get on home and celebrate our first bank robbery together. I think you did good, Slim. Real good."

Charles was pleased with Slim. They had been friends for a long time, and this was the beginning of a good partnership. They had the most important thing going for them, which was trust.

When they pulled up to the house, there sat Rosey on the tailgate of his truck with a notebook in hand.

"Hey, Charles! Here's your notebook. I waved at quite a few folks, including Sherriff Catron. I did like ya said and wrote down the names and times that I saw them. It is kinda fun being you for a morning. Sure didn't take you long."

"Here's a hundred for your work."

"Thank you, Charles. You know how much I appreciate you and all you do for me."

Charles trusted Rosey and knew that he would never tell anyone about being his decoy. He had sworn him to secrecy and promised to always take care of him if he kept the secret of pretending to be him during these robberies. It was a perfect alibi should he ever need one. Reba Sue was the one who had come up with the idea.

Inside the house, Reba Sue was getting ready to go to work. Charles was surprised, as she had called in sick, but she told him that she didn't like getting behind on the transcripts she had to type. She had a good work ethic, and he and Slim laughed about it.

"In the morning, we have to get a newspaper so we can see how much we got," Charles laughed. "It's crazy not knowing exactly what we got until we see it in the paper!"

"When can we go get the money?" asked Slim.

"In a couple of weeks. You come back, and we'll all go together and pick it up.

It will be like a buried treasure."

Slim had purposely placed a rock with a sharp point on the dirt pile, and he had positioned it to point north. If that rock was moved, he would know Charles had been back without him.

Two weeks later Slim came back to Stilwell, ready to get to that money. The newspaper said that the take was $3,596.73. Funny, he didn't remember any change being in the bag.

When Slim got to the house that afternoon, Charles handed him a glass of whisky and proposed a toast with Slim. Reba Sue held up her bottle of Dr. Pepper, and they all took a swig.

"C'mon," she said. "I'm driving while you two are drinking."

They hopped into the car and were on their way to Elkins. They were ready to find out what they had in the bag for real, and it felt like Christmas.

"Now don't get pulled over, Reba Sue," implored Charles. "You got a heavy foot on that gas pedal today, don't cha?"

"Don't you worry about it. I've never gotten a ticket, and I'm not getting one today."

They pulled up to the spot and Slim jumped out to fetch the bag. His heart was racing as he walked up. He wanted to trust Charles. Looking down at the spot, he could see that the rock was still in place.

Back at the house, Charles dumped the bag on the bed, and it looked like a good take. They counted out $4,680, which meant $2,340 each. Not bad for Slim's first day on the job.

"What about the money you paid Rosey, and Reba driving us? Aren't you gonna take out some of my money for that?" asked Slim.

"No, man. I'm taking care of them," said Charles. "Let's go out to the barn, I want to show you this new horse I just bought."

He wanted to talk to Slim alone. He had something on his mind and didn't want Reba Sue included in the conversation.

"I worry about the kids. If anything happens to me, Reba Sue will take care of them. But if I involve her and we both get killed or sent to prison, then they won't have a parent around. Reba Sue loves the planning, so she can just help me with that part. But no more involving her in the actual robbery. Her parents would kill me if anything were to happen to her. She's the best woman I've ever known. Hell, I still can't believe she married me!"

GRACEMONT

Almost a year had passed since Charles and Slim robbed the Elkins Bank, and that was how Charles liked it. By spacing them out, the trail would grow cold, and once that had happened, it was time to hit another one. Besides, he liked to rodeo and race cars and motorcycles during the down,time. His wife had a great job and there was no reason in the world to mess things up by being reckless. Robbing banks was a fun and exciting way to earn a year's pay in just an hour or two.

A bank in Gracemont, Oklahoma was next on their list. They had planned it all out, but it was far from home, which meant that things would be different this time. With the previous banks Charles had been able to get back to Stilwell within an hour or two, but Gracemont was an hour west of Oklahoma City. It was a small town with some good employers and big payroll days.

Charles was getting ready to leave, and Reba Sue was distraught about not going with him. They had talked at length about her not participating, and she had agreed that it was the right thing to do.

"Call me when you get to the city tonight," said Reba Sue.

"I will, honey. And don't worry about me. I'll call you every step of the way just like we talked about. I won't make you worry and agonize over my well-being; I promise you that. I have a bag full of change for the payphones."

Charles pulled Reba Sue to him, kissed her, and then jumped into the truck and left.

He had come up with the idea of building a platform to curl around the engine under the hood of a truck. He could crawl in there and wrap himself around the carburetor. The gas tank behind the seat would be removed, and they would fit a small five-gallon gas can into the space. This would allow the aptly named Slim to be able to fit behind the seat. Hell, he only weighed one hundred and forty pounds. If they went through a roadblock, the only thing the cops would see was a solitary lady driving a truck. It was an excellent getaway plan.

The next morning Charles and Slim met up at the Skyline Restaurant for breakfast. He'd picked the truck up from a friend, who had no idea that he was loaning it out to be used in a bank robbery. Charles filled Slim in on the details of what needed to be done to the truck and he had all the materials needed to customize a platform under the hood. They had recruited Slim's woman, Annabelle to be their driver. She knew of the dangers, but she like Reba Sue, had an urge to participate.

Once at the garage, they prepared the plywood board that would sit around the engine of the '58 Chevy truck. Slim had called Annabelle, and she came over for the trial run. Charles climbed up on the truck and curled himself around the engine. She got into the truck and turned the key. Things looked good, and Charles gave Slim the thumbs up to lower the hood. From inside, Charles could see though the grill of the truck. It was pretty crazy, but he knew it would work. Annabelle drove it around the block. Charles had told her he would bang on the hood if he had any problems. She pulled out on the street and picked up speed. He was riding fine and dandy. After a couple of miles, they heard Charles banging on the hood. She screeched to a halt, and Slim jumped out and rushed to the front to lift the hood. Annabelle came running around the truck, expecting there to be trouble. Charles was laying there grinning.

"I just wanted to be sure you could hear me. And by the way, don't slam on the brakes like that. You about knocked my head off!"

Next, Charles took the gas tank out and replaced it with a small five-gallon army supply tank. They also designed a box to fit the money into under the truck. This was the kind of stuff he loved to do, the preparation. Everything looked good.

"Slim, could you go pick up some bullets for us. I got a ten-gauge shotgun and a 38 special for you to use. Here's some cash. Buy us a couple of nice white handkerchiefs too."

"All right, what are you going to do?"

"I gotta get back to the hotel and rest. I'm exhausted and I need to be well rested for tomorrow."

Turning to leave, Charles called back over his shoulder. "Slim, could you do one more thing?"

"Yeah, what is it?"

"Go steal us a car tonight. Something nice. Make sure you fill it up with gas. I don't ever want to run out of gas in a stolen car again. That almost got me arrested once."

"Sure, Charlie. I'll meet you in the lobby in the morning with everything ready to roll."

"Good night, Slim."

He laid down on the hotel room bed and called Reba Sue. They talked for thirty minutes about the kids, the robbery, and what the plan was for the getaway. Mrs. McBride came on the party line and asked how much longer they were going to be talking.

"Mrs. McBride, could you please wait about five more minutes?"

"You've been talking for a long while."

"We'll be right off here. I promise."

The phone clicked as she hung up. Reba Sue assured him that it was a good plan, and she hoped he would be home tomorrow night. He promised he would be.

He was feeling better now and went over in his mind what he wanted to do once inside the bank and what he wanted to say when he announced that it was a bank robbery. That part was probably the most intense part of the job. The reaction of the people inside was always different. He walked through the hotel room, rehearsing his lines.

"This is a robbery! Do what I tell you and no one will get hurt. Everyone, lie face down on the floor."

He repeated this several times in a stern voice. He was going to own that bank. It would be his for five minutes. He would put those people to work and then disappear.

Charles woke up at six in the morning and went through the robbery step by step in his mind. He showered and dressed in his gray suit. Around eight, he called Reba Sue.

"Charles, please be careful and call me as soon as you make it out safely."

"I'll be very careful today. I feel good, and I got Slim. You know that Slim will take good care of me. I'll be in and out of there in five minutes. You know me, baby. I'm quick as a roadrunner and sly like a fox. We're leaving here in an hour. Takes an hour to get there from Oklahoma City, then it'll take five minutes to hit the bank and thirty minutes to get to our safe place in Anadarko. I'll call you in about three hours, around eleven.

"Charles, I love you."

"I love you too. I'll call you soon."

Slim knocked on the motel room door. Charles opened it and went back to tying his skinny black tie. Straightening his own, Slim put his hat on the dresser and then tied the white handkerchief over his nose and face, turning from one side to the other to get a good look at himself.

"I like this look. Business suits are always a good look. And the handkerchiefs with the sunglasses are great," said Slim.

"Looks good Slim. I like the idea of wearing a suit to rob a bank. When I walk into the bank I want to look like their boss. Because they're going to work for me today!"

Slim chuckled and picked up the flour sacks, starting to put the guns and bullets in them.

They went to Slim's garage to retrieve the 1958 Chrysler Saratoga he had stolen from the airport parking garage the previous night. At the sight of it, Charles gave a long whistle.

"That's a damn fine car. I may have to buy me one next week. I like that you took it from the airport. That's smart."

"I saw the fella get out with his bags and figured he wouldn't miss it for a few days," said Slim.

At that moment, Annabelle pulled up and gave the boys a wave. She had on a big wool coat and knit hat. It was cold and cloudy out.

"You ready, Belle?" said Slim.

"Ready as I'll ever be. Let's get this show on the road."

Charles went over and gave her five hundred dollars.

"Why are you giving this to me now?"

"Because if we get caught, you still get paid, Annabelle. You're working regardless, right?"

"Okay. I don't even want to think about getting caught. Now I'm nervous, Charlie. I wish you hadn't said that."

They pulled out and headed southeast, cautiously going the speed limit. Charles was in front in the Saratoga and liked having someone follow him when traveling in a stolen car. Someone watching his back. After an hour they pulled into

Gracemont. It was a sleepy little town, and there were only a few people out in the cold misty morning. They continued a few miles to the cemetery where they would meet Annabelle later so she could drive them out.

Charles sent Annabelle into Chickasha to rent a room and told her to find a motor lodge. These lodges usually had little cabins that sat alone, which meant that they could get out of the truck without being seen. She stopped at the Indian Motor Lodge because it had cabins far from the office. She asked for a room on the back side and then came up with a good idea. She told the clerk that she was leaving her husband and she might want to hide her car behind the cabin. Of course, he understood and gave her the key to the cabin in the back.

"Would you like for me to check in with you later and make sure you're okay?" asked the clerk, an older gentleman with kind eyes.

"No, sir, I'm sure I'll be fine, but thank you for offering."

She drove around the back of the cabin, parked, and went to the room. It was perfectly located at the very end of the row. She opened a window facing the back side to check what was there, finding only an empty lot. Perfect for the boys to enter through the window. She fetched the suitcase containing their change of clothes and laid them out on the bed in readiness. Then she headed back to the truck and drove the twenty miles back to the cemetery in Horse Thief Canyon. Annabelle pulled through the cemetery gate and traveled up the hill to the gravesites next to a big oak tree where Charles and Slim were waiting.

"Okay Annabelle, you sit tight here. We should be back in less than thirty minutes. If we aren't back in forty-five to an hour, you just go on back home. If we are being chased, we will pull up into that lane just before the cemetery and there will probably be a shootout. I don't want you in the middle of that. You just go on home if you hear any gunfire from that direction. Now if things go smooth—and I believe they will—we'll come back here. Then we'll climb into our hiding spaces in the truck, and you take us outta there to Anadarko and on to Chickasha. That should cover it on the roadblocks. Once in Chickasha we'll split up. They'll be looking for two men in a car and we won't fit that description."

Two days prior, Slim had dropped in to see their friend, Freddy Walker, in Chickasha. Slim gave Freddy fifty bucks to loan them one of the cars from his car lot to drive back to Oklahoma City, which Slim would return a few days later. Freddy didn't ask any questions because he knew Slim was probably up to no good, and the less he knew, the better.

"Slim," Charles said, "get out the bullets and load the guns."

Starting with the shotgun first, Slim suddenly cursed, looking from the bullets to the gun and back again.

"Shit, Charles, I got twelve gauge instead of the ten gauge!"

"Hell, Slim, I'm not going into a bank without a loaded gun!"

"Well, it's a little late to go back to the damn store," replied Slim. "I know you like to carry the shotgun, but how about you use the 38 Special today? And I'll carry the shotgun. No one is gonna mess with us, don't worry."

"I don't like it, and I think you're one crazy son of a bitch. But hell, let's go."

Charles loaded the 38 Special and grabbed two flour sacks out of the back seat. Then he slid into the car. Slim kissed Annabelle and jumped into the car with Charles.

Charles had a bad feeling about that shotgun not being loaded. He didn't like to have any additional things to worry about. He thought about calling the whole thing off but didn't.

Slim pulled the handkerchiefs out and gave one to Charles, saying "Same as last time, right?"

"Yeah, I put the men on the floor and put the women to work. You keep the shotgun on the people on the floor, and I will stay with the people I got working. Let me do the talking just like last time."

"Let's get in and out of there quickly."

Charles pulled the car up right in front of the bank. They pulled the handkerchiefs up over their noses. Charles looked around to check if the coast was clear. They climbed out of the car and took long strides to the bank.

Once inside, Charles saw a man sitting close to the front door, writing on some papers. Pointing his gun at the man's head, Charles loudly called out the lines he had rehearsed the night before. The man looked up from his writing and straight into the barrel of the gun, and his eyes crossed. Then he bent down and got up from his seat, bringing with him a hex barrel 357 magnum. Charles grabbed the gun with his free hand and shot the man. The guy was over six feet tall, and he just stood there, towering over Charles. For a moment, Charles wondered how he could have missed him being that close.

"Why the hell did you do that?" Charles yelled at him. "Now get down on the floor before I kill you."

As the man lay down on the floor, Charles saw blood coming through the man's white shirt. Charles felt sick to his stomach.

Slim yelled, "Why the hell did you do that?"

"Shut your mouth!" He gave the man's gun to Slim and said, "You might need this!"

He walked over to the two ladies that were laying on the floor.

"I need you to get up and come over here with me. Both of you take a sack and start emptying the cash drawers."

They did as they were told.

"Which one of you knows the combination to the safe in the vault?" asked Charles.

"She does," said the younger of the two women, and the older woman frowned at her.

"You get into the vault and get that safe open. Now!"

The older woman was clearly shaking. And when she tried to open the safe it would not open.

"Lady, you better get that safe open or I am going to kill you," shouted Charles.

With tears running down her face, on the second attempt the woman managed to get the safe door opened. Then she loaded the sack with its contents. All the while, Charles could hear Slim cussing and saying something about how sorry he was that the man was shot.

"Now folks, before you call the police, I want you to call an ambulance for this man. I am really sorry that he got shot, but he should have done what he was told to do, and this wouldn't have had to happen."

Once Charles came out of the vault with the full sack, he told everyone to go into the vault, ordering the two ladies to help the wounded man up. He was a large man, and they struggled to lift him and help him into the vault. Charles made no move to help them, and he waved Slim off when he started to approach them. Once they were all inside, Charles slammed the door real hard. He was mad. Slim gave him a dirty look.

Charles moved quickly for the door, and Slim hurried to catch up with him. Looking out of the window, they checked to see that no one was there and then ran for the car. Once in the car, Slim started in on Charles.

"Did you have to shoot the man? Really, Charles?"

Charles saw no one on the street and he peeled out, leaving rubber on the road.

"Apparently you didn't notice the gun he pulled on me. Thank God I reacted as quickly as I did, or we both would be dead. Since you didn't have any damn bullets."

Slim stopped razzing him, realizing that they had come close to a total disaster. Hell, they could both be dead right now.

Charles rolled the window down and stuck his head out, desperate for the cold air on his face. He felt sick. They were going around seventy mph down the road and had not passed a soul, and Charles was thankful for that. The cemetery sign appeared in the distance, and he felt relief.

Annabelle was there waiting and already had the hood up and the seat moved up as far as she could get it. The box was also opened to put the cash into. Charles filled the box and slid it into place. Slim got behind the driver's seat, and Charles climbed up onto the truck and curled around the engine on the platform.

"Remember to stay calm, Annabelle, and if you hear me thumping, get off the main road and pull over quickly."

"I will. Are you okay? Did something go wrong?" she asked.

"Yeah, I shot a man back there. Now please get us out of here."

Annabelle lowered the hood and slid behind the wheel. She didn't see a soul and drove out of the graveyard. She pulled on to the country road nice and easy. When she hit Highway 8, she picked up speed. She nearly jumped out of her skin at the sudden voice from the backseat.

"You're doing good, Belle. Anyone on the road?"

"No! And please let me concentrate, Slim. Don't talk to me," she demanded.

"All right, all right ... But don't you wanna know what happened back there, Belle?"

"No, it will just make me more nervous than I already am."

"Okay."

"Oh, hell no!" Annabelle sucked in her breath and let it out quickly.

They were coming up on a narrow bridge over Sugar Creek and an ambulance was coming toward them from the opposite direction.

Charles could see clearly through the grill of the truck and was feeling better until he saw that ambulance coming fast over that skinny bridge, straight at them. He thought how fitting it would be to be killed in a head-on collision by the ambulance that was headed to pick up the man he had just shot. He couldn't believe that Annabelle didn't slow down and pull over for the damn thing. He just squeezed his eyes tightly shut and rode it out. Somehow Annabelle managed to squeeze the truck past the ambulance.

"If that ambulance is already headed out, then the cops are close behind. Be ready Belle," Slim piped up from the back.,

"I know, I was just thinking the same thing. Sit tight."

They went another three miles before coming upon the roadblock. Charles could see it through the grill, and his heart was racing.

"You be real quiet, Slim," Annabelle whispered. "We got a roadblock coming up." She rolled up to an officer with a cowboy hat on and gave him a concerned look.

"What is happening, Officer?"

"The bank was robbed in Gracemont, and a man was shot. Have you seen anyone on the road?" said the tall officer.

"All I saw was an ambulance, sir. Is there anything I need to do?" said Annabelle.

"No, ma'am, just don't stop for any strangers on the road and be aware. If you see anyone, find a payphone and call the police. Don't go near these men."

"Sure thing, Officer," she said, driving off.

"We did it. We did it, Slim!" said Annabelle. "Now let's get to that motel and get you guys out of here."

She drove through Anadarko and turned west to head to Chickasha. After another fifteen miles, just outside of the town, she saw another roadblock. Right where Highway 81 connected to Highway 62.

"Slim, we're coming up on another roadblock. Be quiet."

"Okay, Belle."

Charles saw the roadblock through the grill, and quietly cussed to himself. He could see two officers there. Annabelle slowly rolled up to one of them but had barely stopped when the officer glanced in the truck and the back and just waved her through without even asking her anything. She was thankful that there were a few cars behind her and some coming the other direction. They were too busy to ask her questions or get a good look at her. She let out a long sigh.

"We did it again, Slim!"

"You're doing great, Belle! Are we almost there? I am getting a cramp all curled up like this."

Before she could reply she heard a banging on the hood.

"Oh shit! Charles!"

Annabelle braked sharply and turned down a dirt road, jumped out of the car and saw smoke coming out through the grill. Quickly looking round, she checked to make sure they were alone before popping the hood. Charles came flying out, smoldering and cursing. His tie had been caught in the carburetor and was on fire. He yanked it off his neck and cursed some more.

"Damn it, that was close! Thank God that didn't happen a few minutes earlier. We would have been caught," he said, jumping back up on the truck and under the hood.

"Close it quick, and get us to the motel, Annabelle."

She closed the hood gently and ran to get back in the truck.

"What the hell happened?" said Slim.

"Charles's tie got caught in the engine and ignited. But everything is okay. We'll be at the motel in just a few minutes. When we get there let me make sure the coast is clear."

"Okay, Annabelle," Slim said, and then he whispered, "Please Lord just get us out of this truck and to a safe spot."

When Annabelle pulled into the Indian Motor Lodge, it was quiet. She pulled by the front desk and saw the clerk sitting on his chair reading the paper. She waved at him, and he waved back. She drove up behind the cabin and yanked the seat up as far as she could. Then she helped Slim out from behind the seat. He unfolded slowly.

"Damn, that was a long thirty minutes cramped in there, but better than thirty years in jail," exclaimed Slim. "Check under the hood, Belle, and get Charles out while I get the sacks out of the box."

When Annabelle opened the hood, she saw that Charles had a worried look on his face. He looked scared. She gave him a hand and eased him out of the engine compartment. He jumped down and Annabelle pointed to the open window.

"Get on in there, Charles. Slim, hurry up with that box. I am going around to the front door just in case the clerk is watching out for me. I'll see you inside."

She got her key and her purse and walked around the corner right into the clerk.

"Oh my, I'm sorry," he said. "I didn't mean to startle you. I just wanted to make sure you were okay. It was taking you a while to get from your truck, so I got a little worried for you."

"Oh, that's all right. Thank you for looking out for me. Now I have to get a few hours of sleep. Thank you again. You're very kind."

Reassured, the older gentleman slowly walked away. Annabelle was thankful he had not caught her with Slim and Charles. That would have been very bad. She opened the door and quickly shut it. Both men were inside.

"Thank God," Annabelle said. "Ten more seconds and the clerk would have walked around the corner and seen us."

Slim grabbed Annabelle and swung her around. "You got us here, Annabelle, and you did a great job."

"You're a damn good driver," Charles added, "except for the part when you didn't pull to the side of the road for the damn ambulance! I thought I was gonna shit my pants."

They all laughed. Then Charles took her by the shoulders and said, "If you keep your beautiful mouth closed and don't tell anyone about where your money came from, I'll give you another three hundred in a couple of months.

She grinned and then said, "Can I help count it?"

"Yeah, throw that money on the bed, Slim."

Slim emptied out the sacks. The guns clattered out of one of them, and Charles picked out the hex-barreled gun that the bank president had pulled on him.

"I gotta go bury this gun. Annabelle, can you please keep these guns in the box under the truck till we get back to Oklahoma City? I don't want anyone to ever find that one. That one ties us to this bank job. I want to be the only one who knows where it's buried."

"You wanna tell me what happened, Charles?"

"No, I don't want to ruin the moment of counting this money. This is the good part. Let's get busy adding it all up and get on out of here."

They put piles of one hundred-dollar bills on the bed. After all the money was counted, they had $11,400, which the two men split into $5,700 each. Of course, Slim gave Annabelle that big tip, and Charles gave her another hundred.

Slim had Annabelle take him to pick up the car at Freddy's place. On the way there, he told her what had happened in the bank.

Once they got back to the motel, Charles left them and headed out to Oklahoma City. He would meet up with them the next day at Slim's place. Slim and Annabelle would stay overnight at the motel as to not give the motel manager any reason to doubt Annabelle's story.

In the morning, the place was filled with state and federal officers. Annabelle went to the office to check out and saw several lawmen checking in. The clerk gave her a receipt and she returned the key.

"Did you hear about the bank robbery up the road? They have brought in a posse of one hundred and fifty men to search for two men. They believe the bank robbers are up in Dead Man's Canyon. You be careful driving out of here. This is the craziest thing I have ever seen! Good luck to you, miss."

A newspaper was laying on the desk, and she asked him if she could have it. He told her sure, and so she picked it up and walked out of the office, just as a crew pulled up with two bloodhounds. She needed to get Slim out of there fast. They should have left yesterday with Charles and not hung around here.

"Slim, we have to get out of here. There are FBI and cops everywhere! I'm going out the front door. After I get around back there, I'll let you know if the coast is clear."

She took the bag of money and put it under her dress, tying it around her waist with her belt. She could not take the chance of getting the box out from under the truck with those guns in it. Peering round, she made sure there was no one in sight and signaled to Slim to climb out of the window.

He crawled back behind the seat fast, and as soon as he was in place she took off. She wanted out of there fast.

Sure enough, there was another roadblock just outside the city limits heading north. Annabelle was so nervous. Yesterday seemed easier than right now. Why hadn't they left last night?

"Annabelle, calm down," Slim whispered. "I can feel you shaking through the seat. Don't you give us away now, girl!" He was nervous too.

She took a deep breath and rolled up to the officer.

"Good morning, ma'am. Sorry to stop you, but we are looking for two armed men. They shot a man and robbed a bank yesterday. Have you seen anyone hitchhiking or walking? We think they're on foot."

"No, sir, I haven't seen anyone."

"All right, then, have a good day."

As she drove off, she let out a long sigh.

"I can't wait to be off the road and back home, Slim."

"Me too Belle. Now we'll be back in the city in just an hour or so.

Charles had not been stopped by any roadblocks leading out of Chickasha. They probably only had enough manpower for the roads leading out of Gracemont at this stage. All the way from Chickasha to Oklahoma City, Charles thought about shooting that man. What if he died?

He needed to get a newspaper in the morning. And the gun had to be buried. So many urgent things to do. He wished Slim and Annabelle had followed him out of there, but he trusted Slim.

Sleep evaded Charles. Every time he closed his eyes, all he saw was the man from the bank. His wide eyes flaring as the gun went off. The blood seeping through his white shirt. He couldn't get those images out of his head, and it wasn't until around three in the morning, that he finally fell asleep.

The next morning, he went downstairs and got a paper. The robbery had made the headlines. Charles read through the story, noting that the police suspected that the criminals were on foot somewhere in the rugged canyon area. They had fifty men searching the rough terrain and had also commissioned a search plane and bloodhounds from McAlister Prison. When the wounded bank president described the robbery, he also told a story of how his father, who was the bank's president back in 1929, shot and killed a bank robber. This made Charles's hair stand up on the back of his neck. If his reflexes had been slower, that could have happened to him.

The story went on to say that the men were described as being between thirty-five and forty years old, dressed in business suits and wearing white handkerchiefs around their faces. It also stated that they discovered that the getaway car was stolen and that they believed that there was no other car involved. They were sure that the two robbers were hiding in Dead Man's Canyon and that they would be apprehended soon.

Charles grabbed another paper. Again, the robbery had made the front page, and this article stated that the officers would keep an all-night vigil around a five square mile section of rugged canyon country near Gracemont, hoping to nab the two bank robbers. It also documented that the injured bank president had been taken to a hospital in Oklahoma City for surgery. The bullet had pierced his liver and he was in a critical condition.

After reading the articles, Charles lay on the bed, reeling from it all.

He called Slim's house and was relieved to hear his voice on the other end of the line.

"Hey, Slim. I'm coming over, so I'll see you in a few minutes."

"All right, Charlie, see you in a few."

Slim went out and got the guns out of the box under the truck. The whole contraption had worked perfectly, and he had to admit that Charles was a natural when it came to planning robberies. He knew his friend would be upset about the shooting.

Charles pulled into his driveway.

"Hey, Slim, good morning to ya. Did you two spend the night in Chickasha?"

"Yeah, we did and in the morning that little motel was full of cops. Freaked Annabelle out. But we got outta there without a hitch."

He pulled the guns and money out of the sack and gave them to Charles.

"I'm gonna bury that hex barrel and pray that man survives. I've never shot anyone, Slim, and it's eating at me."

"Damn, that guy should've done what you told him to do. That crazy son of bitch will live. Don't worry about it, Charlie."

"Did you pick up a newspaper?"

"Yeah, I will go get it out of the car. Get a blanket to wrap that gun in, and I'll get the newspaper article."

Slim wrapped the gun in a pillowcase and handed it to Charles, who passed him the paper in return. Slim gave it a quick eye, skimming down the page.

"It's good that they think we are still out there in the woods. That was the perfect getaway."

"Yeah, that truck idea was good. I'm going to return it to normal out in the garage. Come and help me with it."

"When you started banging the hood and then the engine backfired, I was scared to death that you were hurt." Said Slim.

"Yeah, I bout shit myself."

They both chuckled, then Charles took a serious tone with him.

"Next time I don't care what happens, you keep your mouth shut when we're in a bank. You could have easily said my name when you were chastising me about shooting that fella. Plus, you made me feel worse than I already did."

"I'm sorry, Charles. It won't happen again."

"And that article you just read where that man's father killed a bank robber with that exact same gun. Thank God I had the loaded gun, or I would've been a dead man. That's the stupidest thing I have ever done, and don't you tell Reba Sue about it."

"I won't tell. I don't think I'm cut out for this kind of work. Someone is gonna get killed, and I don't wanna die young. I think you should quit while you're ahead."

"I'm sorry, Slim. I know this business isn't for everybody. I'll take a break and lay low."

They finished up on the truck and Charles was ready to leave. They said their farewells, and Charles headed east out of the city, stopping on a country road in Choctaw, Oklahoma. There, he wiped down and buried the hex barrel pistol. It was an evil reminder of what had happened.

MCCURTAIN COUNTY

A couple of weeks had passed since the Gracemont robbery. Reba Sue and Charles decided to go down to McCurtain County to visit her parents. She missed her family, and she missed living in Golden, Oklahoma. She'd been born and raised in that small town until the day she eloped with Charles on September 11, 1954.

The first night there Charles played dominos with Honey, his father-in-law; Reba Sue's brother, Derril, and her brother-in-law, Streaky.

"Looks like you're doing fine, Charles," said Derril. "Nice clothes and a very fine car to drive. The pipeline company must be paying well."

Reba Sue and Charles had cooked up a story about him working on the oil pipeline to cover up his new profession.

"Oh, Derrill, it's hard work I tell you. Not as fun as being a barber and getting to hang out with the fellas all day. I would trade jobs with you in a heartbeat. And that new car is not mine. It's Reba Sue's car," replied Charles.

"Your hands look mighty soft for working in the oil fields," observed Streaky, looking over the top of his glasses. The other two men looked up at Charles's hands.

"I wear gloves at work, and most times I'm the foreman. Unless we're short of workers, and then I get my hands dirty."

Derril and Streaky knew that Charles had been running whisky when he and Reba Sue lived in the city two years ago, and so they wondered what he was up to these days since they'd moved. He'd probably tell them later, when Honey wasn't present.

Honey told the guys to pipe down and play. He didn't like the conversation, and they caught on quick. Charles wanted the game to be over and they needed to go on home. He was tired of them poking at him.

The next morning, Honey cooked up one of his fine breakfasts for the whole family. Charles felt at home in the Snow house, and even though he knew Reba Sue's mother, Mamie did not like him, she did make him feel welcome. After breakfast, the ladies went shopping over in Paris, Texas.

Honey said he had work to do, and Charles volunteered to help him. They went down to the bottom land and herded the cattle up to higher ground. It had been raining, and Honey was worried that the Glover River would burst its banks and flood the pastureland. Charles was pleased to lend a hand. He loved working cattle and was good on a horse. They had all the cows to high ground by early afternoon.

"Charles, you should really think about becoming more of a cattleman," suggested Honey. "Maybe you give up that working on the oil pipeline."

"Heck, I'd give up working there if it didn't pay so darn good."

"Cattle pays good too though, and you could be home more often to be with Reba Sue and the children. I'm telling you right now your wife and children need you at home, not gone for weeks at a time," said Honey with a firm tone.

"I appreciate your concern, Honey. I know you're right. I'll think it over," Charles replied. He knew that Honey was always straight to the point. And the point was ... don't screw this marriage up.

They loaded up the horses and headed back home. They had a mutual respect for each other. Honey knew his daughter was strong willed and he thought they were well paired. Mamie on the other hand tried for years to run him off and suggested other young men for Reba Sue before they married.

It was early in the evening when Charles told Reba Sue he was going to see some old friends and he would be back later that night. She frowned, but said she was all right with it. Some of her girlfriends were coming over, anyway.

Charles headed toward the Little River Tavern, where he would find Clark Miller, the bar owner and Billy Black, one of his rodeo rider buddies. Billy was a lanky blond, blue-eyed good-looking young man with an outgoing personality similar to Charles. Clark didn't know Charles very well, but he liked how he bought all the drinks for Billy and anyone else who might walk in the bar. Unfortunately for Clark, it was a slow night.

After the few patrons left the bar, Billy and Charles got to drinking and Charles got a little drunk and started telling stories about bank robbing.

Billy was enthralled and told him that he wanted to rob one with him. Of course, Clark was listening in on their conversation and wanted in too.

Charles told them that he already had his quota for the next six months, but that he would tell him how to do it. He liked the idea of coaching Billy to pull off a robbery and make some money on the side by helping him.

"You need a gun, Billy. Do you have a pistol or a shotgun?"

"I got a hunting rifle."

"If you're serious about this, then you need something better than that."

"Charlie, maybe you can help me get the proper gun I need."

"If you get serious, call me and I'll set you up. But I gotta get home before I'm in trouble with my wife. It's nine o'clock and my mother-in-law will have one more reason to dislike me if I'm not home at a decent hour."

Charles left the tavern. He was drunk, and he drove nice and slow all the way to the Snow's farm. Driving slowly was not something he did very often, but he sure didn't want to wreck his wife's car.

The next couple days were good. They had a family portrait done with the whole family and that was an ordeal getting the kids to sit still. On the last night Reba Sue wanted to go dancing with her brother, Derril and Charles got a kick out of watching them jitterbug to the music. She was incredible, flying through the air like a trapeze artist. Charles loved seeing her happy. This trip was just what she needed.

When it was time to leave, Reba Sue cried a little and told her parents they would be back soon. She wished they could move back here, but she didn't complain. Life was good in Stilwell.

*Front row Marc Ribera, Charles Lee, Mamie Snow
Honey Snow and Susan. Back row-Marcus "Streaky" Ribera,
Barbara Jo Ribera, Derril Snow, Reba Sue and Charles*

Three weeks later, Charles got a call from Billy to say that he and Clark had been talking some more about robbing a bank. They wanted to come up in a couple of days to talk to him about getting a gun. Charles recollection of that night in McCurtain County was a little blurry. He vaguely remembered talking about Billy wanting to rob a bank.

Two days later they showed up at Charles's house, and the three began to plan the robbery of the Valliant Bank, a small bank only a few miles from Wright City. Billy would rob it on a Tuesday, just before payday of the large lumber companies in the area. They would spend Monday mapping out the getaway route. Clark wanted in too, so he was going to be Billy's partner. But they needed a decent gun, and that is where Charles came in. He had a machine gun that he'd bought from a friend in Tulsa. Charles made an agreement with them. They would pay him one thousand dollars to provide the gun and a stolen car to use in the robbery, but Charles wouldn't be involved in robbing the bank.

That evening, the three men went over to his Aunt Polly's jewelry shop in downtown Stilwell. Charles parked down the alley behind the shop, and taking the key, led the guys inside. He warned them to stay away from the jewelry area or he would kill them both on the spot. Instead, he made them stand at the bottom of a ladder that led up to the rafters. While they waited, he climbed up and lowered down a long box. The boys' eyes widened as Charles opened the box and inside was an Owen machine gun.

"Last time this baby was used was World War II," said Charles. "Let's get on out of here before the city cop sees my car here and comes rolling up."

They got into Charles's car and swung by his house to pick up their truck. Charles ran inside and grabbed some cold beer out of the refrigerator, and then headed out to a cabin near Bell Community with the fellas following behind. It was a little place that a friend of Charles owned, and it was a good spot to drink beer and plan the robbery. Once inside, Charles built a fire in the fireplace and got the boys beers. They needed something to calm their nerves and to relax them a little. He was about to give them a coaching session.

"Now, when you get in there don't fire this thing if you don't have to. You want to keep things quiet."

"I understand," said Billy "Keep things calm and in control. I sure don't want to shoot anyone."

"Now you have to direct the women to empty the drawers and open the vault. And when you first speak, be very clear. You say, 'This is robbery, and I mean business!' Practice saying it."

"This is a robbery, and I mean business! This is a robbery! Get on the floor!" said Billy.

"Good. That's real good. Now when you're inside the bank the most important thing is to get in and out quickly. And if anyone gives you trouble, you shut them down fast. I am not saying kill them, but if you have to, hit them with the gun butt or yell at them. Get them all down on the floor quickly. Tell them to get face down on the floor except for a woman or two to help you sack the money. Once you get the money and you're ready to get out, make them all go into the vault and lock it. Look outside and make sure no one is on the street. Be patient and wait. Then make your move and get out of there. Don't peel out, just pull out slowly like you belong there. Then get out of there and hide the money. Change clothes fast and destroy everything linking you to the crime. Burn it, bury it, just get rid of any evidence that would connect you to the crime."

They talked more about the details of what would happen afterward, and then Charles left them to sleep in the cabin. He had to get home to Reba Sue and the kids.

"See you in the morning," said Clark.

"Sure. I'll be here around nine. I'll show you how to shoot that monster," replied Charles as he headed out.

The next morning when he got to the cabin, the guys were up drinking coffee. They needed to get some bullets for the tommy gun. Charles didn't want anyone seeing them purchasing ammunition in Stilwell, so they drove the hour and a half to Fort Smith. The atmosphere in the car was electric, and emotions were running high.

"You guys wait outside while I go in and get the bullets," said Charles.

He put on his sunglasses and went into the store and was in and out in less than five minutes. Jumping back into the car, he gave Billy and long hard look, and announced that he would need a different appearance.

They went a couple of doors down from the sporting goods shop to a clothing store and bought a raincoat, slacks, a hat, and some brown slip-on shoes. Billy looked completely different; it was a transformation. Charles was nodding his head, looking him up and down. He started peeling some money out of his own bank roll. He paid for the clothes and the ammunition, viewing it as his investment in this deal.

"Can we go shoot it now? I really want to shoot that tommy gun," said Billy.

"Yeah, let's go over to this place I know," Charles replied.

Charles took them barreling down some dirt roads out to the middle of nowhere. He drove down to a creek and a bluff area and pulled over.

"Now, when you shoot, I want you to shoot into that bluff over there," said Charles.

"You shoot it first, Charles. I want to watch you shoot it," Billy said.

Charles loaded the clip, then snapped it into place and in one smooth motion he fired, making a stream of bullets hit the bluffs. Ceasing fire, he grinned and held out the gun to Billy.

"Damn, Charles, you looked like Al Capone firing that gun," said Clark.

Billy held up the tommy gun and fired into the bluff.

"Oh my God! That is powerful. That is so damn powerful," he whooped. "You got to shoot the gun, Clark."

"No, I don't care to shoot it."

The boys and Charles loaded back into their car and took Charles home. He told them he would drive down to McCurtain County and steal a car for them and charge them a thousand dollars of the take. They could either return the gun to him or buy it for two hundred dollars, but if they chose the latter, the deal was that they had to get rid of it immediately.

"This is the kind of gun that gets people's attention," warned Charles.

As Charles was getting ready to leave, Billy took Clark aside and asked him what he thought about Charles stealing a car for them. Clark told him that it was fine with him. He had no idea about how to steal a car, so best to leave that up to Charles. The plan was for Charles to drive his own car down and help them get this deal figured out. They were on the road and the gun was in the back of their car, which made Clark feel nervous.

Charles went straight home afterward and called Reba Sue at work, telling her he had to make a quick trip out of town and that he would be back in a couple of days. She didn't take this news well, but she couldn't do anything about it. Charles did whatever Charles wanted.

Charles pulled into Wright City around two o'clock in the afternoon. The little town had not changed much, and he was tempted to pull over and say hello to Archie, an old friend that he saw walking down Main Street, but he stopped himself. He did not want to be seen here today. He drove straight out to the beer joint. He picked Clark up and they started planning on how to get a car for the robbery.

They drove east out of Wright City, and Charles informed Clark that they would be driving for a while. It was not a good idea to steal a car close to home. Together, they headed to the little town of Boswell. Upon arriving, Charles noticed a large group of cars at a small church as they went by, and so he turned around and headed back.

"Charlie, you ain't gonna steal a car from folks while they're at a church, are ya?"

"Well, it would be an easy take. Most people leave their keys in their cars."

"Lord, I don't want to steal one from a church parking lot."

Charles was bothered by what Clark had said, so he made a U-turn and headed toward Durant.

"I think I'll go to a car lot and ask to test drive a car," suggested Charles.

He pointed back over the seat and said, "Hand me that hat back there and give me those glasses in the glove box."

Clark reached back onto the seat and grabbed a gray wool fedora. He opened the glove box and pulled out two sets of glasses, one with clear lenses and the other with darker ones.

"I need the dark lens glasses, please," said Charles.

"It is pretty bright out," said Robert.

"Yep, but they are also part of my disguise. You sit down the block and I'll see if I can get the car salesman to let me take a car without him riding along, if so, I'll give you a wave and you follow me. If he wants to ride along, you'll see me go by and know to come back for me."

Clark dropped Charles off a couple of blocks from the car lot and drove away, then he parked down the street.

Arriving at the lot, Charles walked up to a 1958 Buick. It would be fast enough for a getaway car. The salesman was inside talking to another man, which Charles thought could be either a good thing or a bad one. Hopefully, the other customer would distract the salesman's attention, allowing Charles to get in and out of there quickly. He approached the two men and called out to the salesman.

"Hello, sir!" said Charles in a heavy East-Coast accent. "I'm looking to buy that '58 Buick, but I want to take it over to my mechanic friend. Could I take the car over to him? I can leave you a deposit of fifty bucks."

The car dealer just turned and grabbed the keys off a hanger and tossed them to Charles with barely a look in his direction.

"Go ahead," he said, "but I need you back here before five o'clock."

"Sure thing, I'll be back by then, sir."

He drove off the lot and headed east with Clark following him.

He knew of a lane that led to an old, abandoned house outside of Valliant, he pulled the car behind the house and out of view. Then he hopped in with Clark, and they went back to the tavern to pick up Billy. They drove up and down all the back roads to figure out their trip from the bank and back to Little River Tavern where Billy would toss Clark the money bag. Then Billy would head over to Billy Bell Trail where he would run the stolen car into a ditch or a tree on the untraveled road and leave it there. He was to cut through the woods to a cemetery where Clark would come and pick him up after he had buried the money in a pre-dug hole outside the tavern.

The route was established, the plan was set, and now they were ready.

Tuesday morning came, and Charles went over to Billy's place at eight o'clock, finding his friend making his way through multiple cups of coffee.

"Slow down on that coffee, Billy. You'll be a nervous wreck!" warned Charles.

"I like to drink coffee in the morning to wake up."

"Slow it down. You'll need to have calm nerves," Charles warned him. Charles had known Billy as a badass bull and bronc rider. He was starting to worry about him becoming a bank robber, but it was too late to pull out now.

Billy wore a shirt and tie with dress slacks, an overcoat, and the gray fedora with a colorful green feather in the band. Charles thought that he looked good. Once Billy tied the hand-kerchief on and he was wearing the sunglasses, no one would be able to identify him. They were ready to roll.

"Remember," said Charles, "if you get caught don't you breathe my name. You're the ones that want to do this, so don't bring me into it."

"Charles, I promise you we will not tell a soul about you having any part in this," Clark assured him.

Billy swore that he wouldn't flip on him. If he was caught, he'd take the rap.

"Oh, and afterward, don't go around spending a lot of money, or you'll get caught. That is always the hardest thing to do, you have to wait and let time pass. We'll talk more about this after you get that bank robbed. I'll see you guys in a couple of days. Remember don't talk about it, and don't go spending the money until enough time has passed."

Charles headed out of town toward Stilwell. As he drove, he wondered if Billy would be able to pull it off. Then he had second thoughts and started to doubt himself and why he was even doing this.

Clark drove Billy out to the stolen car. Billy put the gun in the back seat under a blanket he had brought, along with the two pillowcases for the money. The bank was not far away from the tavern, so it would be a short drive once he was out of the bank.

Clark looked over at him and felt the need to reassure his friend.

"It'll go fine. You got a damn tommy gun on you, man! Nobody's gonna mess with you."

Billy grinned, but he could feel his nerves jumping.

"I'll see you in less than an hour, Billy," Clark reassured him. "And if I don't … Well, hell, I'll know you took off with all the money."

They both chuckled.

"Go on, Clark, get on out of here. I'll wait ten minutes and then leave. I don't want anyone to see us driving out of here."

What Billy really wanted was some time to compose himself. Once Clark had gone, he lit up a cigarette and took a quick swig from a pint of Jack Daniels he had. He needed some liquid courage right now. To calm himself further, he spent a few minutes practicing his script. Charles had told him to do this and had given him some extra advice, "Think of yourself as the boss, who needs to order his employees to do a job." Charles also stressed staying calm. It would not be wise to lose control. That was how people got shot. Billy thought carefully over what was about to happen as he put the car into gear and headed to Valliant.

He pulled up to the bank. It was a cold day and there were not many people out on the street. He looked around and pulled the handkerchief up over his face, slipped the sunglasses on and placed the tommy gun in one of the pillowcases. Stepping out of the car, he headed straight into the bank, yanking the pillowcase off of the gun and pointing it right at a man who was moving away from the tellers' counter. In a loud but trembling voice, Billy announced his arrival.

"This is a robbery, and I mean business! Everyone, go around the counter and get down on the floor face down, and no one will get hurt."

They all did as he said. He pointed the gun at a man and ordered him to withdraw all the money from the vault. He tossed him one of the pillowcases and the man did as he was told. Billy could see him shoving the money into the case. Then he nudged a woman lying on the floor with his foot.

"Ma'am, I need you to get up and empty the tills into the sack please."

She promptly did as he said. Everything was going well.

Just then a man walked in the door, and Billy spun around, pointing the gun at the customer.

"Get down on the floor! This is a robbery and I need you to get down on the floor next to these other folks right now!"

The man did as he was told. *Damn*, Billy thought, *there sure are a lot of people in here. I need to get the hell out of here.* Just then the man came out of the vault with the sack full of money.

"Sir, I even put the silver in the sack. I didn't know if you wanted it or not but it's in there."

"Now, folks, you all get up and go into the vault. Don't look at me please."

They all did what he said. The lady was finishing with the last teller booth. She put the full sack down on the counter, looking very frightened. She backed away from the bag of money and walked into the vault with the others.

"Now, y'all have done good. Stay in here for five minutes," said Billy, slamming the vault door. He grabbed both of the sacks, only to find that the one from the vault was incredibly heavy because of the silver. He wished he had made the man take it out, but it was too late.

He peered outside and saw that there was no one around and went out to the car. He threw it in reverse and pulled out. He wanted to speed out of there so badly but kept his cool and cruised right out of Valliant.

The sacks were full. Billy couldn't help grinning as he looked in the rearview mirror. He laughed out loud but then became serious; he wasn't out of this yet.

Once he hit Highway 98, he picked up speed and got to the turn off within five minutes. No one was following him. He got to the Little River Tavern, and Clark was waiting outside. Billy tossed him the two sacks full of money. Clark's eyes widened and he let out a hoot as Billy sped off toward the landing at Tucker Lake, it was less than half a mile from the tavern. He threw the gun as far as he could into the lake. Then he drove up Billy Belle Trail and ran the car into a tree close to the cemetery as planned. He went into the woods across the road and walked up toward the old cemetery they had staked out. He changed out of the dress clothes and hat, put them in a pile and set them on fire. It was freezing outside, and he took another swig of Jack Daniels to warm himself. After most of the clothes had burned, he put out the fire and hiked up to the old cemetery and waited for Clark to come get him.

Meanwhile, Clark was taking the sacks to the hole he had dug the day before. The one with the change in it was heavy. Just as he approached the hiding hole, he stumbled and heard a loud crack as a searing pain tore up his leg.

"Oh, damn it! I think I broke my damn leg!" he cried.

He crawled over and put the money in the hole he had dug. He tried to walk back to the truck but felt excruciating pain shoot through his leg. It was a bad break, and there was no way he could drive his truck to get Billy. That truck clutch was not easy to press with a good leg. He crawled back to the bar and called his little brother, Kenneth and to ask him to come to the tavern. He had Kenneth take his truck to pick up Billy because he didn't want him to shoot at his little brother when he saw a different vehicle approach. Tears were running down Clark's face as his little brother drove off; he had just involved Kenneth in a bank robbery. He knew that this was not going to be good, he could feel it in his gut. Minutes before he had been ecstatic at the surreal amount of money in front of him, and now he was in sheer terror at the prospect of endangering his little brother.

Kenneth pulled into the old cemetery, and out of the woods came Billy. When Billy saw that it was Kenneth and not Clark picking him up, his heart raced. All kinds of thoughts ran through his mind.

"Clark broke his leg," Kenneth called out. "He couldn't come and get you, so he sent me."

"Okay, did he tell you anything else?" asked Billy.

"Yeah, he told me that the pair of you just robbed the Valliant Bank."

"Great, that is just great," muttered Billy.

"I'm going to put that down to the pain he was in. He's in shock, and I bet he doesn't know what he's saying," Kenneth said, before pausing and adding, "And hell, if you guys did that, I don't want to know anything about it."

"That is good, Kenneth. Let's just keep it that way. I don't want you involved in this."

Kenneth put the truck in gear and drove them back to the Little River Tavern. It was a very quiet ride. When they got to the tavern, Billy asked Kenneth to wait in the truck for a few minutes and to take Clark to the hospital after he had left. Kenneth nodded his head and lit a cigarette.

"How'd it go?" Clark gritted his teeth in pain.

"It went well. Everyone did just as I told them to. No one gave me any trouble. I think the tommy gun really helped. It scared the shit out of them. Now remember, Charles said that the important part is the getaway, so we got that part done. We're good."

"When are we gonna count the money?" asked Clark.

"How about right now. I'll lock the front door to the bar."

"You know where I hid it, so go get it and then get me to the hospital."

Billy went to fetch the money, bringing it back a few minutes later and pouring it onto the pool table. He started counting the money, increasingly astounded at how much was in the sacks.

"Oh my God, Clark! We got a lot of money here."

He put it in stacks of five hundred. After he finished counting, he let out a low long whistle and turned to his friend.

"Seventeen thousand dollars. Plus, all these damn coins," said Billy in awe.

"That's really good!" Clark laughed through his pain. "Where is Kenneth?"

"Outside. I told him to wait for a few minutes and to take you to the hospital. But first, let's go over the plan. I'll put the money back in the hiding place. Once you return from the hospital and a couple of days go by, we'll meet back up. Trust me, we are partners in this. I'm not going to steal from you. I'll see you in a couple of days. Don't go near that money."

Billy helped Clark hobble out to his truck and jumped into his own. He took the back roads home. They had done it. It wasn't perfect, but so far, they had gotten away with around seventeen thousand dollars.

After a couple of days had past, Billy went over to visit Clark. He had a cast on his leg and he was hating being laid up at his house.

"I probably don't deserve half of this Billy, since I didn't even go inside with you."

"It's okay Clark. We did it together and we're partners. Now do like Charles told you. Don't go spending any for at least a couple of months."

Billy had been thinking about all the things he was going to buy with his share of the money. He already had a little farm picked out on the north side of Stilwell. He wanted to get out of McCurtain County, and now he had an opportunity. He could hardly wait to go over to Parrott's Jewelry Store and pick out a nice big diamond for his girlfriend, Lori Lynn. They were going to have a wonderful future together.

Billy had gone out and got a newspaper every day since the robbery. He remembered Charles talking about how fun it was to read about your robbery the next day, and it sure was surreal to hear the story told by the folks at the bank and to find out what the witnesses remembered about the robber. He had made the headlines.

GUNMAN ARMED WITH TOMMY GUN ROBS OKLAHOMA BANK

A masked gunman armed with a tommy gun robbed the Farmers State Guaranty Bank today of an estimated $15,000. Bank president J.W. Teeters made the estimate.

The thug escaped in an older-model, heavy car believed driven by the confederate.

"This is a stick up and I mean business," Teeters quoted the thug as saying.

The man was in the bank five to ten minutes before fleeing to the north or west.

The bank employees said the gunman was about twenty-five to thirty years old nd wore a handkerchief over his face. No one was injured, and no shot was fired. Roadblocks were thrown up in the southeast Oklahoma area.

The article was short and not very interesting, but the next day the articles were more compelling.

VALLIANT GUNMAN, LOOT STILL GONE

The search for the cool gunman with a crisp voice who took $17,275 from the Farmers State Guaranty Bank on Tuesday is still on the loose. Officers said that the wrecked car could be a decoy, or it could have been wrecked and caused the gunman and his driver to flee into the woods. They are inclined to believe the men fled into the heavily wooded area.

Perhaps, the bold gunman is holed up in the cold, foreboding foothills of the Kiamichi Mountains with nothing but two sacks of coins and currency to keep him warm.

The getaway car was found on a gravel road about ten miles north of Wright City near the old Indian village of Aliksha.

Or perhaps he slipped through a cordon of Texas, Oklahoma, and Arkansas lawmen and sped safely away for parts unknown. Sheriff Art Monday had very little to go on. If a man knew the back roads of the Kiamichi foothills, he could have gone any direction and escaped that way. Fifteen FBI and OBI Investigators were concentrated in the Hugo and Wright City area today.

Billy got a big kick out of reading the articles out loud to Clark. They laughed and talked about the robbery and how things could have gotten ugly.

Billy still couldn't believe that so farthey had got away with robbing that small bank in Valliant, their neighboring little town. But it felt too close to home. People around town were talking about the robbery and how many of the men that worked at the lumber company didn't get paid that week. That part was hard to listen to, as many of their friends and family worked for the big lumber company. It was the largest employer in the county. They hadn't considered the impact the robbery would have on the community, and it made them feel ashamed. People close to them were affected, and everyone got behind on paying their bills and buying food for their families. This robbery took a toll on the folks in the area, and this ate at the men.

When Billy had walked inside the bank and took charge as Charles had told him to, he felt invincible. Taking control of the employees as though they were his own was what Charles had advised. Even though it was the most intense feeling that he had ever experienced, he didn't think he ever wanted to do it again.

Clark had taken his money and buried it down by the fishing hole on the river close to his house. As soon as things cooled down, he wanted buy cattle and land.

In the end, Clark only managed to go two months before he started spending the money. He bought a section of land in the richest bottoms near the Glover River. The people of the town took notice. There were slippery tongues wagging in McCurtain County. Shit was about to hit the fan.

FRENCH AND MCGLINTY

Clark was driving along State Highway 70, south of Little River near Wright City and unbeknownst to him he was being cautiously followed by agents, Frank French and Vandy McGlinty of the FBI.

Clark pulled down a lane off the highway where fishermen would often park in order to head on down to the river. It was easy for French and McGlinty to pull down there as there were people coming and going. They watched Clark head into the woods in broad daylight. McGlinty held up his binoculars and studied their suspect.

"It's looking good, French. He's got a shovel, and I don't think he's digging for worms to fish with."

"Let's give him a minute to dig, then we'll move in on him," said French.

The county sheriff had been tipped off by a nineteen-year-old rodeo cowboy who wanted the $300 cash reward for sound information on the whereabouts of the money stolen in the bank robbery. The young cowboy had told them that he was pretty sure that Clark Miller had robbed that bank in Valliant, as he had overheard him talking to his younger brother, Kenneth about it. He also heard him saying that he was going over to the sale barn next week to buy cattle for the new farm he had just purchased.

Agent French had done some research and decided it was a good tip. Clark lived close to Valliant and did not have the sort of job that would allow him to purchase a farm. He seemed to be as good a suspect as any, and there were no other leads. French decided to start tailing him and sure enough, it had paid off. Clark had led the FBI right to the money. This was going to be a huge success for French, what with the spate of unsolved bank robberies in Oklahoma recently. The director of the FBI, J. Edgar Hoover had made it known that he wanted these bank robberies to stop and the robber to be apprehended. French desperately needed to solve this one.

French was thirty-eight years old and had been with the FBI for ten years. He was a tall, dark-haired man, with piercing brown eyes. He dressed in dark business suits with slender ties and chain-smoked Lucky Stripe cigarettes.

That afternoon, his partner McGlinty had arrived from Muskogee to lend a hand. He was one of the best FBI agents French knew, and he was extremely intelligent, with excellent intuition when it came to solving crimes. He looked deeper into each and every crime scene and was able to find evidence that no one else would notice. McGlinty was a former military intelligence officer, at the age of fifty he considered his current line of work to be his retirement job. He didn't look or act his age and French had seen him run down a twenty-year-old the week before, and that kid had a good lead on him. McGinty was short in stature with reddish blond hair and green eyes.

Stealthily, they approached Clark, just as he unearthed a glass jar filled with bills. French had his gun drawn. When Clark turned and saw them, he knew instantly that it was all over. These guys were feds, not the local sheriffs.

"Looks like we have a buried treasure here. Clark Miller, you're under arrest for the robbery of the Valliant State Bank. You may remain silent, you have the right to speak with an attorney," announced McGlinty. French cuffed Clark and put him in the car. On the drive to the McCurtain County jail,

French let Clark know that they knew his little brother was involved and that Kenneth would be picked up by the sheriff later that evening. French knew that when there was a younger sibling involved, the suspect would often plead guilty and tell all. Presuming the arrestee had a heart that is. But French could tell by Clark's reaction that he was soft, and that his little brother was important to him.

"He had nothing to do with this," cried Clark.

"We both know that's a lie. We've already sent someone to pick him up. We will see what your brother has to say about all of this," replied French.

"What if I told you about the two others that were involved? Would you keep my brother out of this? Two for one seems like a good deal to me."

"We might be willing to make a deal. But you must tell us where the machine gun is. Our case has to be solid for me to let your brother out of this," added McGlinty.

"I need you to go back to the area we were just at," sighed Clark.

French turned the car around and returned to the lane by the river.

"Turn left here instead of going toward the river," Clark said, looking out of the window as they headed up over the hill and toward a pond. "The gun is at the bottom of that pond."

French smiled and looked at McGlinty, who promptly got on the radio and requested that they bring the equipment out to drag the pond for the gun. While they waited for the sheriff's men to arrive, French took the jar with the money and began to count it.

"Clark, I only count five hundred dollars here," said French.

"I'll take you to the other hiding place."

"There better be a lot more than this. There was over $17,000 stolen."

"There were three of us to be paid. I bought a truck and put money down on a farm. I don't have much left. I was planning to buy cattle for the farm at the sale barn tomorrow."

After the men showed up to drag the pond, French took Clark and drove toward Wright City. Clark directed them to his new farm just outside of town. He led them to the barn where he dug up another jar. It contained $600.

"You're still short to the tune of $15,000," said French.

Clark wanted to throw up. Everything was going to hell.

"When we get to the station, I want you to tell me everything you know. I'll question your brother also. Your stories better match up or you're both going to prison," said French.

Clark started to have an anxiety attack and begged to have a smoke. French took the cuffs off Clark and lit a cigarette and handed it to him. The kid was young, and the agent noticed that his hand was shaking badly as he took the cigarette. *Not cut out for bank robbing,* thought French. *This was going to be an easy case.*

They pulled up to the McCurtain County courthouse in Idabel. McGlinty got Clark out of the car and took his arm and led him inside, where they went into a room and started the interrogation. French started in on him.

"Ok, start from the beginning and tell us everything if you want a deal for your brother. And please acknowledge that you're doing this of your own free will. If we believe you and you're straight with us and give us information on others involved, we'll try to get your sentence reduced. But we are not promising you anything until we hear the complete story," said French

"I'll tell you everything," replied Clark, forlornly.

And he did. He told them about Billy and how they devised a plan to rob the bank. About how he had sent his brother to pick up Billy and every detail of what happened.

Then French said, "I think you're leaving something out. And if you want to save your little brother you will tell me right now what you're hiding."

French had used those very words with many criminals in previous interviews, and they had worked repeatedly. The con would give him more details and more names, hoping for leniency.

After a long pause, Clark gave them the grand prize. He gave French the name, Charles Parrott. Clark told them about each of the bank robberies Charles had committed. He even gave them Mad Dog's name. But he didn't go into the details that Charles gave him about successfully robbing a bank. He didn't tell him about the disguises, the people impersonating him while he was robbing the banks or the change up places such as the cemeteries. And he didn't need to. They were thrilled with the information he provided.

"Now we're going to talk to your little brother. And if the stories match up, we turn Kenneth loose," said French, turning and walking out of the room with McGlinty.

"Damn, we have hit the jackpot!" said McGlinty.

"Three banks he said, besides the Valliant job," French shook his head and added, "There could be more banks, and he is just giving us these to get his brother out."

"Let's just go with this, French. What we have is solid. We will get to this Parrott guy and break him."

They questioned Kenneth and his story matched up with Clark's. They weren't going to release him just yet, but the kid's respectful manner and how angry he was with his older brother told the agents that Kenneth had integrity and by no means approved of what his older brother had done.

McGlinty got on the phone to Golden Reed, an agent out of Northeast Oklahoma.

"Golden, we got some bank robbers for you to pick up over at a farm in Stilwell."

"Damn it, McGlinty, it's late. Can I pick them up in the morning or is this a situation that needs immediate attention? If not, I'll call the county sheriff and ask him to take me to the farm early in the morning."

"Sure, Golden, but if someone gets to them and lets them know we are on to them, they will run. You better be there before dawn," said McGlinty.

"I'll call you in the morning when I have them."

Golden hung up and turned to his wife. "Damn, this is a long week. I've got to go to Stilwell and pick up Charles Parrott and some kid named Billy Black. Looks like I'm taking them to Idabel in the morning, Dottie. Hard to say when I'll be back."

"So much for spending time together. I'll tell Joey you got called in. We will do something together next weekend," said Dottie.

She smiled and kissed his neck. She knew what she signed up for when she married a G-man. She had been a bootlegger's girl when she met him, and she liked this calm lifestyle much better, even if it meant he would be gone just as often as a bootlegger. They had fallen in love five years ago when he was questioning her about her boyfriend, who'd just been killed by a Texas underworld hitman.

Golden knew Charles Parrott from Oklahoma City. He had been a bootlegger around the same time as he met Dottie, and he knew that he had run liquor for Jay Chaney. Dottie had worked for Chaney too, but that was a long time ago. Golden hadn't seen Charles in five or six years.

"Guess Charlie graduated from bootlegger to bank robber," said Dottie. "It's too bad. I thought he went straight when he left Oklahoma City."

Around five in the morning, Golden and the county sheriff pulled up to the Parrott farm south of Stilwell. Golden knocked on the front door of the brick home, and after a few minutes an attractive blonde opened the door.

"I have a search warrant and an arrest warrant for Charles Parrott," said Golden.

"He's not here. Why are you looking for Charles?"

"Do you know where he is?"

"You didn't answer my question. I'm his wife, and I have a right to know why you have a warrant to search my home."

"We have reason to believe that your husband was involved in a bank robbery in Valliant, Oklahoma, and we are here to search for evidence and transport him to the McCurtain County jail."

Reba Sue did not look pleased with that statement and asked to see the warrant. He handed it to her, and she read every word. *She is buying time*, thought Golden. This woman was smart, and he could tell that she knew her rights. He would do everything by the books with this one. After she read the warrant, she opened the door and let them in. Golden and the Sheriff searched every room looking for Charles, but he was nowhere to be found.

"When was the last time you saw your husband?" said the sheriff.

"Now, Sheriff Conway, you know Charles. He's always off at the horse shows or rodeos this time of year. He took off a couple of days ago, and I have not heard from him since.

I believe he said he was going to Joplin, Missouri yesterday. I can have him call you and come turn himself in when he returns."

Reba Sue did her best to get them to leave. She knew that Charles and Billy were down at the chicken house sleeping off a hangover because she had kicked them out the night before when they had returned drunk. They were too loud, and the house was no place for their drunken antics. The chicken house was almost finished, fully bricked and brand new. She had thrown a couple of pillows and blankets at them around midnight and sent them down the hill so the children could sleep.

"We'll just take a look around, ma'am," said Golden.

She hoped the agent wouldn't go down to the chicken house to search for them. As they moved away from the door they headed toward the barn, and Reba realized that they would search the whole place. Then they'd find out she'd lied to them.

Reba Sue hated lying, but that was exactly what she had just done. She was becoming a liar, a thief, and a criminal for him. She didn't care what the FBI or the police thought. She slammed the door hard, hoping it would wake Charles and Billy. She wondered why the dogs weren't barking.

Looking out of the window, Reba could see that Golden had dropped down onto one knee and had called the dogs to him as soon as he walked away from the house. *Damn*, she thought, h*e knows exactly what he is doing. Calling off the warning signals from dogs.* That was why she hadn't heard a sound until the knock on the door. She turned and got the coffee out of the cabinet. It was going to be a long day. Charles was going to Idabel. This was worse than just an arrest, there was also the shame involved. Reba Sue used to work at the county courthouse in

Idabel, and everyone there knew her family. News traveled fast in McCurtain County, and her parents would find out quickly. Her poor momma would be so mortified, and her daddy would want to kill Charles.

"Damn it to hell!" she yelled.

Golden walked through the barn, admiring the surroundings. It was a real nice place that Charles Parrott had. There were some fine saddles in the barn, high dollar bridles and blankets. He looked over and saw a bucking rig, chaps, and spurs hanging on the pegs in the tack room. He motioned Sheriff Conway toward the chaps and spurs. There was also a nice leather duffle bag that held items a cowboy would use. Golden finished searching the barn and then headed down to the chicken house. It looked brand new. He pushed the door open and there on the floor were two men sleeping on some blankets with a couple of pillows. They were fully dressed as if they had just come in from the rodeo. One of them had mud on his back, where he had probably been thrown from a horse or bull. They still had their boots on. A bottle of Jack Daniels was laying nearby. They hadn't been here long, Golden thought, so maybe the wife was telling him the truth. Maybe she didn't know they were down here.

Golden pulled out his gun and nudged the cowboy with mud on his back.

"Charles Parrott, you're under arrest for the robbery of the Farmers State Guaranty Bank in Valliant, Oklahoma."

Charles raised his head and squinted his eyes, looking up at the agent and Sheriff Conway.

"I don't know what you're talking about," said Charles.

"Are you Billy Black?" asked Sheriff Conway to the other man.

"Yeah, I am," replied the cowboy.

"Billy Black, you're under arrest for the robbery of the Farmers State Guaranty of Valliant, Oklahoma," said Golden.

"You gotta be kidding me!" exclaimed Billy.

Golden motioned to the sheriff to cuff them while he held the gun on them and told Conway to take Billy, and he would take Charles separately to Idabel. He didn't want them together for a second. He thought he saw Charles look at Billy and motion with his lips for him to be quiet.

"I want to speak to my attorney," Charles said. "Tell my wife to call my attorney please."

Charles looked toward the house and saw Reba Sue in the window, looking at him and she was shaking her head. He knew she was furious with him. She had told him she didn't like him helping the guys rob that bank. He should've listened to her.

"I'm not telling your wife anything," Golden replied. "She knows where we're taking you."

Charles felt sick to his stomach. He was in trouble. Big trouble. Someone had talked and his guess was Clark or Kenneth. Billy had been with him for the last couple of days, so it wasn't him. He felt like dogshit. He was hung over and beat up from the night before.

His mind was cloudy from the whisky and painkillers. He had ridden one really mean bull by the name of Death Wish. After the bull had finished with him, it propelled him hard onto the red clay arena. Charles had yelped and thought his collarbone was broken. He had taken several painkillers throughout the night.

Right now, though, he needed a clear head and the only way he was going to get straightened up was to sleep. He stretched out on the back seat and closed his eyes. He was going to be very cool with the feds. Stay cool and say nothing. He wondered what they knew.

"So, Charlie, I see you have graduated from bootlegging to bank robbing," said Golden from the front seat.

"I really don't want to talk to you without my attorney present. I'm tired and I'm going to sleep. I had a hard night at a rodeo. After I wake up and have some coffee, maybe we can chat. Just small talk though because I have no idea why you're arresting me. Okay, Golden?"

"All right, Charlie."

Golden didn't know Charles well, and it didn't look like he was going to get to know him on the 170-mile trip to Idabel. *This guy was clever*, he thought. He would sleep off whatever he was on, which was probably a combination of booze and barbiturates from what Golden could tell. When he stopped to get some food, he would try again to get him to talk.

In the other car, Sheriff Conway had somewhat of a confession from the young cowboy before they even got past Sallisaw. The sheriff told him that his friend, Clark Miller, had already informed them how the robbery happened. He also told Billy that they had the submachine gun that he had thrown into the pond. At that, he confessed to robbing the bank in Valliant. But he did not incriminate anyone else. He even cried and said that he did it so he could marry his high school sweetheart and start a good life for them in Adair County.

He was feeling like shit. He was still high and drunk. He felt like he was in a twilight world, trapped between day and night. But at least he'd left the others out of it. He would take all the blame. He wondered what the cops knew and if Kenneth or Clark had been caught with money. His stash was still buried, and he would lie and say he spent every penny in Mexico or something. He was not going to go to prison and have nothing to show for this. His future did not look good. Despairing, he shut his eyes and tried to drift off to sleep. He was exhausted.

Golden pulled over in Poteau, Oklahoma at a diner, and Conway pulled in behind him. Time for breakfast and to refill their thermoses with coffee. Golden would leave Parrott in the car with Conway keeping an eye on the two while he ordered them breakfast. He turned and saw that Charles was awake and still looked bleary eyed.

"Want something to eat for breakfast?" Golden asked.

"Yeah, that sounds good. How about some biscuits and gravy?" said Charles.

"I'll be back in a minute," replied Golden. "Hey, Conway, what do you want? Billy, you want breakfast? I'll go in and order it for us."

"Pancakes and bacon for me," said Conway.

"Same for me," said Billy.

Golden went inside and made the orders, showing the waitress his badge and telling her that he would need to take the plates outside to the feed the men in custody. That would be safer than bringing them in, he told her, and that got her curiosity going. He went back out to the cars and the waitress brought coffee out to them on a tray a few minutes later.

A few of the folks in the diner were staring out the window at them and sipping their coffee. Conway took Golden aside and told him that Black had admitted to robbing the Valliant bank, but that he said Parrott had nothing to do with it.

"Damn, Conway, excellent job! Ever think of joining the OBI?" said Golden quietly, adding, "Now, we don't want Parrott to find out he confessed. I want to see if I can get anything out of Parrott first."

The waitress brought the plates out and after they were done, they got back on the road to Idabel. Golden turned to Charles and asked, "You want to tell me how you know this kid, Billy Black?"

"Sure. I've known him for a while through rodeo riding. But I don't know him well. We rode over together to the Joplin rodeo."

"So, you didn't hook up with him down there and help him rob the Valliant bank?" asked Golden.

"No, I didn't, and like I told you before, I don't want to talk to you without my attorney present so end of discussion," said Charles.

Golden wasn't going to get anywhere with Charles Parrott. He turned the radio on and looked at Parrott in the rearview mirror. Charles was smiling and gazing out the window as if he didn't have a care in the world. This guy didn't seem like he was guilty of anything, and Golden wondered why the other guy in McCurtain County would lay blame on Parrott. French would brief him when they arrived in a couple of hours.

THE BEST ATTORNEY
THAT MONEY CAN BUY

As soon as Charles was driven away, Reba Sue called the best attorney in McCurtain County, Mr. Tom King, who was a good friend of her father's. Thankfully, her father had a lot of connections in McCurtain County, and Reba Sue knew she was going to need the best attorney that money could buy to get Charles out of this. She left a message with King's secretary to say that she was Honey Snow's daughter and that she desperately needed his help.

Tom King was educated at Vanderbilt and had moved to Idabel to be near his parents. His clientele were primarily the owners of the large lumber companies in the southeast of the state, along with several well-known politicians who had trouble with legal issues. So, while he was the best in the business, Reba Sue was unsure whether he would accept the case to represent an alleged bank robber. She could only pray that her father's name would strike a chord.

When King returned Reba Sue's call, he didn't even ask her what the case was about. Instead, he simply told her to come to his office the following afternoon so that they could discuss how he could help her. He apologized that he didn't have any time to talk about the case right at that moment.

Reba Sue drove down to Idabel the next day, and on the way, she gave careful consideration to what she should tell King. She knew exactly what had happened regarding

Charles's involvement in the bank job, and she knew that what he had done was stupid. She had told him so beforehand, adding that she didn't like it. But Charles didn't listen, and just did it anyway. Drinking and telling stories was a bad combination, especially to guys too young and ignorant for their own good. So, Reba Sue ruled out the truth; it would not be a good story to tell King and would only make Charles look like a complete idiot.

Arriving in Idabel, first she went and booked a room across the street from the courthouse and then went to see Charles and ascertain exactly what the charges were that had been leveled against him. Reba stood on the courthouse lawn, staring up at the four-story building where she had been employed five years ago. Her first proper job after graduating from high school had been here, and her mind flooded with memories.

Now, years later, here she was standing before a place she used to love, preparing to go inside that courthouse to bail out her wild, criminal husband, all the while wondering what in the world, she was going to tell her parents. They probably already knew. Word traveled fast in this county.

As she walked in, she saw several people she knew, but she left her headscarf and her sunglasses on, doing her best to disguise who she was. She didn't want to speak with anyone that morning, with the exception of Charles and Mr. King.

One of the sheriff's deputies led her back into a small room to visit Charles. Once inside, she removed her scarf and sunglasses and did her best to act cool. She sat there for ten minutes. While she was waiting, she noticed a tall man standing in the room across from her. He was a fed. She was sure. She had read enough true crime magazines to know the way these guys worked, and so she was well aware that he was watching her, assessing her behavior and demeanor. She knew he would want to question her. He was not the same agent who had come to the house; he was nowhere in sight. So, the games had begun. She and Charles had already talked about what would happen if he got caught, which could have been at any time, as they well knew. The plan was that Reba Sue would act as though she had no idea of what was going on. She was to be kept out of it.

Charles entered the small room with a serious look on his face, one that Reba Sue had never seen before. He was frightened.

She got up and went to him, holding him closely.

"I've called Tom King. Everything's going to be okay, Charles. I love you."

"Tom King, you say? I thought he was a state senator," replied Charles.

"He just moved back home from D.C. and has opened a private practice. He's a very good friend of Daddy's and so I called him yesterday morning after they took you. We are meeting this afternoon. If he takes the case, you'll see him soon. I pray he'll represent you."

"These federal agents will probably want to talk to you."

"I don't have to talk to them. I know my rights."

"That's my girl. There is a ten thousand dollars bond to be paid so I can get out of here. If we pay it in cash, we get it back, but if we get a bail bondsman then we pay fifteen percent and never get it back," said Charles.

"That's a lot of money to never get back, but if we post cash, they will be suspicious as to where we came up with that kind of money. I'll see what I can do," said Reba Sue, her voice beginning to tremble. "I better go."

She held him tightly before leaving, and while up close to him she whispered in his ear.

"Do you have any money hidden?"

"Yes," he murmured back. "Dig under that burn barrel behind the barn. But be careful. They may be watching you."

He kissed her on the cheek and turned to leave the room.

From across the hall, French watched them interacting. *That girl was cool as a cucumber*, he thought. *She hardly showed any emotion*. As she left the room, French approached her.

"Are you Mr. Parrott's wife?" said French.

"Yes, I am," replied Reba Sue.

"Could I ask you a few questions? I'm Agent French with the Oklahoma Bureau of Investigation," he said.

"No. If you would like, you can speak with my attorney. I'm on my way to talk with him right now. I have no reason to speak with you Mr. French unless you suspect me of some crime. My husband needs representation, and I really must go."

And with that statement, she tied her scarf under her chin and slid on her sunglasses. He stood there speechless. She looked at him over the top of those dark glasses for a moment, turned, and left.

Watching her go, French was acutely aware that she was going to be tough to interview. She was clearly intelligent. He resolved to leave her alone for the time being, especially since he wasn't even sure if Parrott was guilty of the crime. First, he would find out if Clark Miller was telling the truth or not. After all, he could be lying to save his younger sibling. So far only Miller had implicated Charles, and this had not been corroborated by Billy Black.

Reba Sue left the courthouse as fast as she could, unable to get out of there quickly enough. She was livid at Charles. It had taken all of her resolve not to hit him across the head and tell him what an idiot he was, but she had known to stay calm. It was important to put on an act in front of the agent. Walking away from the building she was fuming and could feel the old Snow temper building up. She needed a pill to calm her down before she exploded. It would not be good to meet King in a furious rage.

She walked over to her hotel and went inside and took a Librium. She laid down on the bed and waited for the pill to take effect. She had never taken any medication besides aspirin before she married Charles, but now she enjoyed the calming effect of Librium when she was anxious or couldn't sleep. Plus, it helped her to deal with that bad temper of hers, and right now she was acutely aware that if it wasn't for those little pills, she would probably have a nervous breakdown. She had three hours to kill before she met with King, so she lay on the bed and went over in her mind what she would tell him.

Reba Sue felt more relaxed after her rest, but she didn't like the task at hand. She was anxious about going to see her father's friend, but she knew he was the best attorney and that was what they needed. She said a little prayer and freshened up her makeup. She left the hotel and walked the two blocks to the attorney's office.

"Reba Sue Snow … my, my, you've gotten more beautiful since I saw you last. You're a woman and not a teenager anymore," said King.

"Why thank you, Mr. King. That's very nice of you to say."

"Come into my office, and let's talk."

Reba Sue walked into the office and looked at the pictures of King in Washington with well-known politicians. She went to one of the chairs across from the attorney and sat down, trying her best to keep her composure.

"Reba Sue," King began, "I saw that Charles was arrested yesterday, and I'm sure that's what you're here to talk about."

"Yes, it is. I'm not quite sure what happened, but I know that Charles is innocent," lied Reba Sue.

"I'll go over and speak with him as soon as you leave, then I'll see what the charges are. I'll do my best to get him cleared of this," King reassured her.

"You mean you're willing to take the case?"

"Of course, I am. Your daddy and I go way back. I'll do my best to convince your daddy that Charles is innocent. I'm sure you're concerned about what your father's response will be to all of this."

"Thank you, Mr. King. How much is the retainer to hire you?"

"Nothing, Reba Sue. For right now let's just get the wheels turning and we will work out payment later."

Reba Sue started to cry. King came over and put an arm around her shoulders.

"It'll be okay, Reba Sue. Just let me take care of this."

"Thank you. I have to get going. I need to fetch the bail money and get Charles out, and then head back to Stilwell. I have to go to work and make sure the children are okay. Can I wire you the money and you bail him out for me?" Reba asked through her sobs.

"Yes, I can do that for you."

"Okay. I'll go back to the courthouse and tell Charles you're coming soon," said Reba. "Oh, one other thing, Mr. King. The FBI are wanting to question me, but I informed them I did not have to talk to them without my attorney present. Do I need to speak with them? If I don't, will it make Charlie look guilty?"

"You did the right thing. I'll speak with them and tell them that you have had to return home to care for your children. Go home, and I'll call you tomorrow and let you know how we are doing. Don't worry too much. I'll take care of this. I promise you."

Reba Sue rose out of the chair, thanking him for being such a good family friend. She slid the sunglasses on and left.

Reba Sue walked back over to the McCurtain County Courthouse and slipped in a side door. She went quickly up the back steps all the way to the top floor where they kept the prisoners. After four flights of stairs, she leaned against the window on the last landing, her rapid breathing making her mouth dry. She looked down at the courtyard and saw the federal agent, French, speaking with another man. Then he got into his car and left. Reba Sue gave a sigh of relief and carried on up the last set of stairs to the top floor. Once inside she found the soda machine and got a couple of Dr. Peppers. The county sheriff saw her and told her he would fetch her husband, so she walked over to the visiting room and sat down to wait.

When Charles came inside the room Reba stood up and gave him the cold bottle of soda. He held her and kissed her on the cheek.

"Listen, I don't want to stay here long. That fed—French— just left and I don't want to be here when he returns. I need to get back to our kids and my job. I've been to see Mr. King. You now have the best attorney that money can buy."

"That's good, Reba Sue. I know it wasn't easy for you to do that because of your daddy."

"It went better than I thought it would. He didn't ask me about anything. Which is good since I don't know anything. This is all so crazy," she said, in case they were overheard.

Charles winked at her and said, "We will clear this up and move on with our lives."

"I feel so awkward here. I just want to get home as soon as I can Charles. I have never been so embarrassed in my life. I gotta go."

"I'm so sorry, honey."

"I'll get the money as quickly as I can for the bond. I am going to wire it to Mr. King who will bail you out. I don't want to come back here right now. Perhaps never."

"I love you, Reba Sue. If you need help raising the money, call Dougal. He'll help us out. He is a good friend, so call him if you need to, honey."

He held her and kissed her on the forehead. "It'll be okay. I promise you. I'll get this cleared up. I love you."

"I love you too. I gotta go," she turned and left down the back stairs.

"Hey!" the jailer called out, "you gotta use the front stairs."

She ignored him and carried on the way she was going, knowing that he wouldn't pursue her. He had prisoners to keep an eye on.

"She knows her way around this courthouse," Charles piped in. "She used to work here. She won't do no harm."

Reba Sue got into her car and headed north out of Idabel. She was too ashamed to face her parents. She had always known that the day would come when Charles would be arrested, but it had never entered her mind that it would be in McCurtain County. No matter what happened, her parents would never forget this. Her poor mother would be mortified, and her sister would be furious. The only one who probably wouldn't mind would be her brother, who would in all likelihood just laugh and brag about his criminal brother-in-law. She had no idea how her daddy would feel about all this.

RAT FINKS

Clark Miller told Agent French everything. He told him what banks Charles had robbed and who he robbed them with, but he left Reba Sue out of it. He knew her family and didn't want any part of that Snow temper coming after him or his kin. Plus, he wasn't completely sure if Reba Sue had actually participated in any of the bank robberies, only that Charles had called the female getaway driver "my woman," but knowing Charles that could have meant any one of a dozen women at any given time. Miller found it hard to believe that Reba Sue would be in on it, because that girl seemed as strait-laced as they came. Everyone in McCurtain County knew Reba Sue Snow.

Two weeks before they were arrested, Billy had called Clark to brag about how much fun he was having with Charles in Stilwell. The pair were making plans to rob another bank, and Billy said that he was going to be a rich man. He crowed about all the women he met through Charles, and how going to rodeos with his friend was the best time a man could hope for. Every Thursday through Sunday they would travel from one rodeo to another.

While in jail, Clark had a lot of time to think about how everything was going to play out. He'd taken the public defender that was offered. After speaking with him, he was advised to give the agents whatever information he could. Since he had no other previous offenses, it was likely that they would take it easy on him. But Clark didn't care what sentence they gave

him, however long it was, providing Kenneth was safe. Despite
that, he wanted to know what was going to happen. The court
date was a few weeks away, and Clark wanted this terrible
part of his life over with.

After Clark gave the agents the information they wanted,
they released Kenneth without bail and dropped all the charges
against him, but Clark didn't know how things would play out
for himself. He thought about Billy and wondered if he would
plead guilty. He knew that his accomplice would be furious
with him because he idolized Charles and had plans to rob
more banks with him. Clark hadn't told the feds about that.

After arriving at Idabel, Billy Black was taken to the interrogation room and Agent French was not getting much out
of him. Black had slept off the drugs and booze on the last
leg of the ride over from Stilwell and was better prepared to
face questioning. French could tell that the kid could go far
as a criminal. He acted cool and calculated when under fire,
and French could easily picture him welding a tommy gun
around a bank and ordering people to do as he said. Maybe
this kid had robbed other banks in the past. The employees
had said that the robber was very calm, almost as if he had
done it before. Looking at his suspect, French didn't notice one
nervous movement. Black sat there and smoked a cigarette,
talking as if they were old friends and he was as comfortable
as he could be. He claimed that it was his idea to rob the bank
and that he had wanted the money in order to move away
from McCurtain County and buy a farm. Then he had planned
to go to Wright City and ask his girl to marry him. He was
trying hard to sound like a sap. While he confessed to seeing
Charles during the week of the robbery, he claimed that it was
just social drinking and men carrying on together. Charles had
nothing to do with the robbery.

"Clark is just trying to make things up to get his little brother out of this. It's my fault for giving him that heavy bag of coins and then him falling and breaking his leg. Clark should never have sent his little brother, but he's just a coward who couldn't kill a flea. I'm willing to confess to what I did and pay for my crime."

"Where is the money?" said French.

"Here's where I really screwed up. I told you I robbed the bank because I wanted the money to buy a farm and marry my sweetheart. I took that money and went down to Old Mexico to stay away for a while until things cooled off. But hell, I got robbed while down there. A whore drugged me and took my money. I don't remember anything except waking up in the hotel room to find it all smashed up. She had found the loot and had taken it. Fortunately, I had hidden a couple of thousand back home, so when I got back, I took that money and started spending it. I only have eight hundred dollars left."

"I don't believe you," stated French. "Where is the money?"

"The eight hundred dollars is in a bank in Stilwell, and the rest is with an expensive whore in Mexico."

"I still don't believe you, Billy."

"I am sorry about that, but it's the truth. I don't know what else I can tell you."

French left the room and turned to McGlinty, saying, "That kid is smart, and he is lying to me. Although he's a damn good liar. I have a real hard time reading his body language. He won't give up the money. And he won't give up Parrott either."

"Leave him in there for a while. Make him sweat it a little and then I'll go in," replied McGlinty.

They let him sit there for two hours and then the older agent went in.

"Want a cold drink?" said McGlinty, handing Billy a cold soda.

"Sure. That's very kind of you."

"Now, Billy, you need to give me some more information on where the money is. And Parrott's involvement in this robbery. There is no way that you took that much money to Mexico. And why would Clark Miller be compelled to snitch on Parrott if he had nothing to do with the robbery? Just tell me why that is?"

"I am telling you the truth about the money. I took that much to Mexico because at first, I wanted to buy a big ranch there. And I could buy over a thousand acres for the price of one hundred here in the States. The night before the transaction, I was set up. I think the son of the ranch seller set me up, knowing that I was carrying a large sum of cash to make the purchase. I was stupid to carry it across the border, I know that now, but I did and then I was robbed. I was a fool. Later on, I thought to myself, Billy, that is what you get for ill-gotten gains."

"What about Charles Parrott?" asked the agent.

"That's a complicated deal," said Billy. "Clark Miller has always been jealous of Charles, ever since he had sex with Miller's girlfriend. On more than one occasion, too. Charles likes to rib Miller and tell him how hot his girlfriend is. Silly shit like that. Miller does not like it, but what can he do? Charles is a ladies' man and has a knack for charming any woman he wants away from any man. He's a Casanova. Do you know what a Casanova is, Mr. McGlinty?"

"Yeah, I know what you mean."

"Miller is a very jealous type, and I'm guessing he figured he would lie and get Charles involved to get his brother off while also removing Charles from the picture with his girl-friend. The only truth he told was about my involvement."

McGlinty thought this over. The kid could be telling the truth, but hell, who could tell? Criminals lied all the time. For now, they'd take the confession from Black, solving the case regardless of Charles Parrott's involvement.

Reba Sue went to dig under the trash barrel. After a few moments she struck metal and stopped digging, bending down to uncover the metal cigar box. Seizing it, she quickly put it inside her pocket and rolled the barrel back over the hole. She ran back up to the house and opened the box, pulling out the money stuffed inside. She counted out $4,200 dollars and she wondered whether any of it was marked.

Aunt Polly came up with the rest of the bail money. She loved Charles like her own son and had spoiled him ever since her brother Bud had married Odessia when Charles was four years old. Polly was devastated that he was arrested. She knew he'd been bootlegging whisky and sometimes ran with a fast crowd but had no idea he was into anything as serious as bank robbery. She had tried to get him to stay in college when he was young and to make something of himself, but he'd chosen to lead a cowboy life instead. While he made some money at the rodeos, it was not the occupation that she'd planned for him.

Polly thought that Reba Sue was a good girl and had hoped that she would help Charles to become a more mature and godly man, but she was wrong. Reba Sue was the breadwinner in the family, and she let him get away with too much drinking and carrying on.

When Polly contributed toward the bail money, she hoped that the experience would be a wakeup call for Charles. The thought of him being locked up devastated her, and so she went to her former boss, the banker, and got the money.

Reba Sue promised Polly she would pay her back as soon as she could. She was under a lot of stress since her husband's arrest, but three days after he was taken, she had managed to get together the money and wire it to Mr. King. He called her at work to say that he'd received the money, and that Charles would be on his way home that very afternoon. An old of friend of theirs, Jesse Bowling, would be driving him home.

After putting the phone down, Reba Sue decided to do her best to get through the rest of the day. The newspaper article of Charles's arrest was in the local newspaper, and everyone in Stilwell had heard about it. The women in the typing pool kept looking over at her and then at Bud Parrott's office. Her father-in-law was her boss, and it was a stressful time for both of them. Bud's office was located in the far corner of the room, with a glass window. That week Bud had asked Odessia to install curtains in there, and they were up and drawn within thirty minutes of her arrival, giving him some much-needed privacy, but poor Reba Sue had to acknowledge the stares and strange looks from her colleagues as they whispered about her.

While she was sitting there thinking about the phone call and ignoring her workmates, Bud came out of his office and walked over to her, telling her to take the rest of the day off and the next day also. He turned and walked back to his office, and not a single person dared to lift their head as he did so.

Reba Sue gathered her purse and headed out the door. She was thankful to Bud for letting her leave. He was a good man. She raced down the highway to her home. She could have picked the kids up early but decided not to, as she needed time to calm down. Charles would be home soon, and she didn't want to scream at him the moment he walked through the door. It wouldn't do any good, and he would just leave. She took a pill and laid on their bed, wishing that she had never married him and never had these children with him. It was selfish of her to think like that, but she could've had a better life than this and she knew it.

She thought about James Sherman and how he had asked her to marry him. A smart and good-looking man, he was a much better person than Charles. But she hadn't felt the same way about him. She loved Charles.

"Damn you Charles Parrott," she cried aloud.

Lying there, she heard a car pull up and soon after, the front door opened. She stayed on the bed and pretended to be asleep. She was groggy from the pill and was feeling relaxed, thankful that her temper had cooled.

Charles was worried as he entered the house, unsure of how Reba Sue would react. He could only imagine her being extremely upset with him; of that, he was certain. He walked into the bedroom and over to where she lay, admiring his beautiful and faithful wife. Her honey-blonde hair was spread upon the pillow like silk. Petite and fragile, she was curled on her side facing him upon the soft chenille bedspread. She was loyal and would fight like a tiger for him.

He laid beside her and kissed her forehead and whispered how sorry he was about everything that had happened. He would get out of this trouble one way or another. He told her that he appreciated her and thanked her for getting him the best lawyer in McCurtain County.

She laid there quietly and let him have his say. After he'd finished, she softly spoke up.

"Charles, I love you, but if you keep drinking and running your mouth about robbing banks, I'll divorce you. That is why we are at this place. The booze and the bragging will be the end of your career as a bank robber. Now you get yourself out of this mess, and we will go forward from there."

He held her close to him and said, "I'll be a better man. I promise."

"Let's get started on how we get out of this," said Reba Sue.

They spent the next hour talking about Mr. King and the plan for the case. Reba was confident that they would work things out and clear Charles's name. But little did they know that Agent French had been doing his homework and had a lot more information about Charles's involvement in the unsolved bank robberies.

King had called Reba Sue's father, Honey, and discussed the charges against Charles the same day that she had hired him. It was the respectable thing to do. Forget the lawyer/client shit, there was nothing wrong with telling Honey his thoughts on the case, although he would not share what Charles had told him, which was not much, really. He had told Honey that he thought he could get Charles cleared of the charges and that was pretty much the gist of it. Honey asked him if he thought Charles was guilty and his response was, "You never really know what people are capable of."

When Charles Parrott introduced himself to King, he felt a little intimidated. Everyone in Southeast Oklahoma knew King as a high society lawyer who represented crooked politicians and a large lumber mill in the area. He once had quite an illustrious career and now had retired to his own private practice. Charles could not believe that he had such an impressive attorney representing him, and it was all thanks to Reba Sue that he did. His only question was whether King was a good criminal attorney.

"Mr. King, it's a pleasure to meet you. I'm just wondering if you're the right man to represent me," said Charles.

"What about me troubles you?" asked Mr. King.

"I hate to say it, but I am a criminal, Mr. King. There are things that I do that you might not agree with and being as you're a friend of Honey Snow that might stand in the way of you representing me I need a criminal attorney, Mr. King."

"I can understand your concerns, Charles. But I promise you that I can represent you fairly, regardless of my friendship with Honey Snow. I have kept many guilty people out of prison, and I have put many a man and woman in prison. I may be sixty-two now, but I got a lot of fight left in me. You'll see. Are you ready to get started or would you like for me to recommend someone else to you?"

"Let's get started," said Charles.

Charles was completely honest with King. He told him everything that had transpired with Black and Miller. He told him that he had bragged about some other robberies to them as well.

"So, you told them how to rob the bank and supplied the gun and the stolen car," interjected King. "Did the car dealer get a good look at you?"

"No, I was well disguised, and he was busy with another customer. I don't think he would recognize me. I also used a different accent when I spoke to him."

"Where did you get the tommy gun?"

"I found it through a friend of mine and thought it would be a good intimidation factor for the next bank I robbed," answered Charles.

"If it is traced back to the friend, would he lead the feds to you?"

"No, they won't be able to trace it to him. At least, I don't think they will. And he wouldn't lead them to me. We've been friends since we were kids. There is deep trust between us. He knows that when he gets me guns, they cannot be traceable. He knows what I do."

"Okay, the main thing here is to weaken their accusations, so that they can't be substantiated. We will use the angle that Miller is jealous of you, and that he is just trying to get his brother out of trouble. You will admit to drinking with them and that they were really drunk, and you were not. They talked about robbing the bank, and you joked with them and said that this is how you would do it. But never implied that you were telling them how to rob a bank. They are just trying to get a lighter sentence and using you to do it."

"What about the other banks I told them about?"

"Start lining up your alibis, Charles. They are going to have to have proof that you were in those areas at those times. If you have solid alibis, then I think we can beat them."

Charles told King about the alibis he had established for the earlier robberies, and it was at this point that the attorney realized that he was dealing with a serious and professional criminal. He was going to have to put together a good defense and see if he could pull this off.

"I'll call you in a couple of days Charles, and let you know what is going on. I'll find out what Miller and Black are saying about you and will begin preparing for court. In the meantime, just lay low."

"All right. Have a good evening Mr. King."

After Charles left, King began thinking about how he would defend his client. He needed to go over to the jail and see what he could find out about the other two and what they were pleading. Were they testifying against Charles as part of the plea bargain? If they were, then King was going to have a hard time beating this depending on the evidence. He was going to prove to Charles Parrott that he could represent a criminal as well as he could represent a crooked politician.

King went over to the courthouse where he pretty much knew everyone. This helped him in his cases. People liked him. They liked that their hometown boy came back to retire and didn't stay in the big city of Washington, D.C. They were proud of his accomplishments and accolades. It was good for McCurtain County to have him back home. Most of his friends were judges and he liked going to court and fighting for the bad guys for a change. It was a lot more entertaining. Now he was going to see what he could find out about the Valliant Bank case and work out what he was up against.

First, he walked around the courthouse seeing what he could find out. Betsy Stafford, the secretary for the assistant district attorney, was always a good source. They had worked together, and if his timing was right, he would catch her immediately after all the attorneys and law clerks went down to the diner for their lunch. His timing was good. Betsy sat there at her desk with her headphones on, typing rapidly.

"Did you hear that Honey Snow's son-in-law was arrested?"

"Oh, I sure did. And bless Honey and Mamie's heart. Their daughter sure ended up with a bad boy," said Betsy.

"Do you think he did it?"

"Those brothers sure are setting him up for a fall."

"I'm thinking about representing him as a favor to the Snows," said King. "Do you think I would have a chance of getting him out of this mess?"

"You know I can't tell you much being as I work for the other side, but you and I go way back so I'll tell you this … they are setting him up for more than this one. And that is all I am gonna tell you."

"Okay, but you didn't answer my question. Do I have a chance of getting him out of this?"

"Mr. King, I think you could do a damn good job. And I think it will be hard for the jury not to be charmed by you and Charlie Parrott. Now I gotta get back to work."

King turned to leave. "Thank you, Betsy. I think I'm going to take this case on."

He went upstairs to see if the Miller brothers and Black were still locked up or if they had been bailed out and found that they were still in jail. However, just that afternoon they had dropped the charges on the younger brother and set him free. That was all King needed to know. This case was going to be a challenge.

Charles and his lawyer in the preliminary hearing.

Charles was going to be in trouble if Mad Dog was implicated in the Pineville robbery. He had made Mad Dog swear to keep his mouth shut, but it had been Charles who had given the game away by running his mouth off to Black and Miller. They could sell out both Mad Dog and Charles to the feds, and so he needed to find out what he was up against, as a matter of urgency.

Since Miller and Black had both plead guilty, the court sentencing came round. King told Charles to sit tight and promised to let him know what transpired as soon as he knew something.

Charles went over to Aunt Polly's house to phone Mad Dog, just in case the feds were tapping his house phone. He did not want them to hear this conversation and was confident that they would surely not bother with his aunt and his grandmother's phone.

"I got bad news, Dog. I've been arrested for helping some boys rob a bank in McCurtain County. They pled guilty and have given the feds information about me. I don't know what they have said yet, but I wanted to give you a heads up, so that you can be ready if your name gets brought up. Shit, I did something really stupid, and I'm really sorry. I got drunk with these boys one night and I think I may have mentioned one of our robberies to them. I don't think I involved you, but I just want you to have the heads up on this. If by any chance they bring you into this, I'll pay for your attorney and bond. Or if you want to take a trip to Old Mexico, I'll spring for it. Hell, it was my drinking that may have made a mess of all of this. Damn, I was such a stupid idiot! I am sorry."

"Hell, Charlie, I'm the one who talked you into robbing the first one. If I have to ride this one through to the courtroom, then I will. Maybe it will take them a while to find me out here in California," replied Mad Dog.

"Reba Sue has hired me the best attorney in the state of Oklahoma, and if needed he will represent both of us at my expense."

"Shit, Charles. Let's just see what happens, okay? You find out what we're up against and call me."

"Hopefully they won't have anything on us other than hearsay. I don't care what they said, there's no way they have any evidence. And I don't see them just taking those boys' word. Surely, they'll just put it down to two young bank robbers who are trying to get less time by snitching on another guy. I'm going to plead innocent, and so are you if you're charged. They need proof to find us guilty, so I reckon we can beat this."

"I reckon you're right, Charlie."

"So just don't talk to anyone and be careful if you think you're being watched. I know that they are tailing me. They don't seem to be on to you, and I hope it stays that way. If I need to talk with you, I'll call you from a secure phone. I don't want their surveillance of me to lead them to you. And remember, if you get arrested, contact Tom King's office and I'll have him ready to bail and represent you if needed. Get a pencil and I'll give you his number to call."

"Don't worry, I'll sit tight, and if they snitch, we will deal with it then."

"I think we are going to be okay. I'll get back with you soon."

Next, Charles had to contact Slim. He was his best friend, and he hated the fact that he may have ruined things for him.

"Hey, Slim, I got bad news. You know that I got a big mouth, and this time it has gotten me in a whole heap of trouble. I got drunk and bragged about the robberies."

He went on to tell Slim what had happened.

"Charlie, you need to learn that you can't trust everyone. There are too many people who would willingly snitch rather than do their own time."

"I know I was stupid. But I have a good lawyer, and I called to give you his number, just in case the feds pick you up."

As he had done with Mad Dog, Charles gave Slim the number for King's office, reminding him not to say a word to the feds without his attorney present.

Slim swore that he would not say a word and then, after a pause, he added that he was scared.

"Me too, Slim. We will get through this. I promise I will get you out of this. Now start finding some alibis for the days we robbed Gracemont and Elkins, and make sure they are solid. And don't tell anyone what really happened. Watch yourself, Slim. They may start tailing you."

"Just keep me updated. I'll go about my business as if nothing ever happened."

"Sounds good. I'll talk to you later."

It wasn't long before Charles found out that Miller and Black had told the feds everything they could possibly tell them with the exception of bringing Reba Sue into it. Charles had thought better of Black and wanted to kill him for this betrayal, but what had he expected? Charles had been fed to the wolves. People would do whatever they could to save themselves.

King had seen this coming and had warned Charles about it. In the end, Miller and Black pled guilty and each got eight years in prison. Charles had pled innocent at his preliminary and was still out on bail awaiting his trial, but King assured him that while the boys were on their way to prison, they would most certainly show up at his trial to testify against him.

Charles would be going before the US District Court of Eastern Oklahoma in Muskogee. Now was the time to start thinking how he was going to avoid any jail time. He had to get out of this. Things were looking bleak, but he had a good lawyer on his side. If he went to prison, he would lose his wife and children. Reba Sue was strong, but she might give up on him He couldn't bear the thought that his kids would think he was a terrible man. That would kill him.

King had suggested that they should partner up with another attorney in Muskogee, Paul Hammer. They would have a better chance of winning. Hammer had connections and was known to be a rabid defense attorney. He also had a good track record of winning criminal cases. Another benefit was that just ten years before he had been the assistant district attorney for Eastern Oklahoma, which was the same court that Charles was about to face. Both King and Hammer were former district attorneys who enjoyed a good and challenging case. Charles agreed that the addition was a good idea and was willing to pay whatever it took to get out of this mess. Hell, he would even rob another bank if he needed more money.

He was out on ten thousand dollars bail, and his family was mortified. His mother had slapped him so hard across the head that his ears rang.

"You're just like your real father, a criminal! I brought you into a good upstanding family and this is the thanks that you show them."

Charles begged her to tell him who his real father was, but she adamantly refused. This haunted Charles, as he was desperate to know what it was that had made him like this. Whose blood ran through his veins? Clyde Barrow perhaps? Or maybe Pretty Boy Floyd, who just happened to die the year Charles was born and was buried near the hills in Sallisaw,

Oklahoma. Maybe Pretty Boy was his father. Odessia had insinuated that his father was a criminal, but that was all she would ever tell him. That and the fact that Charles looked just like Floyd.

Odessia was especially upset because they had a big formal dinner to attend the next week after the preliminary court date. Charles and Reba Sue were supposed to be going, and Odessia knew that her son was the hot topic in town. The bank robbery was all over the newspapers and would make for an embarrassing night.

The day came for the formal dinner, held in honor of a member of the Adair County Welfare Department, Mr. Jacks, who was retiring after twenty-two years. He was a social worker who was well liked by everyone in the office and would be sorely missed. The party was held at the Stilwell Café in the back room, and the buffet table was loaded with fried chicken and lots of sumptuous side dishes and desserts, including Odessia's beautiful strawberry cake. There were about ten employees in the welfare department, and they all brought their spouses to the dinner.

Reba Sue didn't want to attend the party, but Charles forced her to go. She hated the small-town gossip about Charles being a bank robber.

Running a little late, they pulled up to the café and Charles said, "Reba Sue, everything is going to be fine. I don't care what those people think, and neither should you."

"That's easy for you to say. You don't have to work with them five days a week. In fact, you don't even work Charles. I do," replied Reba Sue.

Charles got out of the car not saying a word and walked around and opened the car door for her.

"At least you have manners," she muttered, getting out.

When they walked into the back room of the cafe, all eyes fell upon them, but to their surprise the people were smiling. It seemed that no matter what Charles did, people liked him.

The outcome of the trial was on a lot of people's minds in Stilwell, but Charles acted as if nothing had happened and went about his merry way at the party. He had the men laughing and the women's attention.

Bud looked over at his stepson and turned to Odessia, stating that Charles should have been a politician or a lawyer.

"You should have never bailed him out when he stole those tires," she replied angrily. "He was only fifteen years old, and you impressed on him that he could get away with committing a crime."

"Now don't blame me for that. I just didn't want him to sit in jail. But heck, maybe you're right. I should have made him face the consequences."

"It's too late now. And he seems to think he can do no wrong," Odessia replied, looking at her son. He was standing with his arm around his wife, and he was smiling and laughing.

"Let's just get through the night and have a nice dinner and send off for Mr. Jacks. Then we can dig into that beautiful cake you baked. That was real nice of you to do that," said Bud, planting a kiss on her forehead and walking away.

Odessia looked at her son, laughing and carrying on. Reba Sue looked as uncomfortable as her mother-in-law felt. That poor girl had her hands full with Charles. *She probably regretted marrying him*, thought Odessia. Now they had two kids and while she was working at a good job, he ran around the countryside calling himself a rodeo cowboy. Odessia decided that she was going to have a talk with Reba and tell her to lay down the law with Charles. He had to get a real job. She didn't know if Reba Sue would listen to her, but she was going to give it a try. She knew that Charles was smart and could most likely get honest work, but Reba Sue just let him do whatever he wanted and that needed to stop. Surely with the court proceedings coming up he would realize that he needed to look more like a law-abiding citizen.

Charles acted like he always did. Confident and a little cocky were the impressions that he left on most people. People were looking at him a little differently all of a sudden, wondering whether or not he was capable of robbing banks. Charles reckoned that most of them probably thought that he was.

In the end, the dinner went well, and if people were curious about Charles Parrott's escapades, then they certainly didn't show it. The tight knit group that worked for Bud and with Reba Sue were like a second family to them, and Reba Sue was relieved that the evening had gone as well as it did, and she was thankful to her coworkers for being kind to her.

Charles and Susan 1958

Reba Sue was a force on the basketball court 1952

Easter 1961

Charles and Reba Sue 1956

Charles, Toni and Charles Lee in Alaska

ALL HELL IS
BREAKING LOOSE

I t was a cold January morning, and Reba Sue and Charles were snuggled up together in their featherbed, fast asleep. The night before they had stayed up late listening to records and talking. Charles had teased his wife by saying that she would not be getting enough sleep and should probably call in sick to work the next day so that they could spend it together. That was their plan until a banging on the front door woke them at six in the morning.

"Damn it! Who could that be at this time?" cried Reba Sue.

"At this time of the morning, I would have to guess that it's the law."

Reba Sue covered her head in the blankets and let out a groan as Charles got out of bed and headed to the front door. When he opened it there stood two men dressed in suits standing with the county sheriff. One of the suited men he recognized as OBI agent French, and he had a gun drawn.

"You can put the gun away. I'm not some kind of dangerous criminal. My wife and kids are inside, and I don't want you to scare them," said Charles.

"Charles Parrott, you're under arrest for robbing the People's State Bank of Westville, Oklahoma," announced French.

"We also have a warrant to search your home," added the one who said his name was Agent McGlinty.

"Can I get dressed and send my kids and wife to my mother's house first?"

"Sure, you can. But I don't trust you right now to go back into the bedroom without one of us accompanying you," said French with the gun still drawn.

"Come inside."

"I'm Agent French, and this is how this is going to work. No one is allowed to leave just yet. Your wife could take evidence out of this house. Now I don't want to upset your children, so after you get dressed and get your kids up, I'll let your wife leave with them."

Reba Sue came into the room in her robe. As soon as she saw the men in suits, she asked them whether they had a warrant to enter her home.

"Yes, Mrs. Parrott, we do," said French.

"Then let me see it," she demanded.

He handed her the warrant to search the premises and also the one for her husband's arrest, both of which she examined carefully before throwing them back at French.

He bent over and picked them up off the floor, taken aback by her behavior. She was a tiny little woman with a big backbone.

"Mrs. Parrott, we will allow you to get dressed and take your children to your mother-in-law's home while we search the residence," offered Agent McGlinty.

"Oh, you will allow me, huh? I'm not leaving my home, and you can do whatever it is you do while I'm here unless you have a warrant for my arrest," stated Reba Sue.

"I know you're upset, Reba Sue," said the sheriff in a kind tone. He knew this family well and hated having to accompany the agents on this task.

Reba Sue ignored him and said to French, "I am going to get dressed and get my children up. Please refrain from speaking to them."

"First, I need my partner to accompany Charles to get dressed while you wait here," French said, turning to his partner and nodding. "Go with Charles while he gets dressed. I don't want any funny business here."

McGlinty followed Charles into the bedroom and stood there, waiting patiently while Charles took his time picking out his clothes. As he went into the bathroom to brush his teeth, the agent started to follow him.

"Are you going to watch me piss?" enquired Charles.

"Yes, I am afraid I am," said McGlinty, turning his back.

"I'm going take a shit too."

"Fine, I'll be outside the door."

A few minutes later Charles came out looking like he had shaved and smelled of Old Spice. They went into the living room to find that the children were now up and sitting in their pajamas in their little rocking chairs. Their eyes were glued to the television, watching *Captain Kangaroo*. Reba Sue had made coffee, making a point not to offer any to their uninvited guests. She poured a cup and handed it to Charles. He took a sip and put his arms around his wife and kissed her on the cheek.

"Charles, let's take you out to the car," said French.

Charles's four-year-old daughter, Susan ran up to him and wrapped herself around his legs.

"Daddy, where are you going?" asked Susan.

"I have to go for a ride with these men, Honey Girl," said Charles.

"Okay," she replied, and wandered back over to continue watching the TV with her older brother, Charles Lee.

"Daddy, will you bring me a Baby Ruth bar when you come back?" hollered the boy.

"Yes, son, I will."

"Thanks, Daddy! I'll be a very good boy today." The little red-headed boy smiled.

Once outside, the agents handcuffed Charles and placed him inside the sheriff's car, and shut the door. Watching from inside, Reba Sue was pacing like a cat. She wondered if she should have left the house with the kids, but she didn't want to leave these men in her home. She and the kids would ride this out. She told the children it was time to get dressed and sent them off to pick out their clothes. She dressed hurriedly while the men were outside, so that she could get back to the living room before they returned.

Once French came back inside, he informed Reba Sue that they were about to start searching the home. She looked at him as if she couldn't care less and sat down on the sofa with a movie magazine.

The men started in the back of the house, systematically going through the bedrooms. They spent a long time in the big closet that held all of Charles's clothing and shoes, but they did not bring anything out with them. From over the top of her magazine, Reba Sue was keeping a close eye on them. If they found anything, she would know it. The kids asked what the men were doing, and so Reba told them that they had lost something and thought that maybe their daddy had it. It was like a treasure hunt, she told the children, and they had to look in several houses for it. They accepted this story and went back to watching *Mr. Green Jeans and the Captain*.

The three men carried on searching, with one heading off to the garage and another into the kitchen to rifle through the cabinets. French came into the living room and started looking around. There in front of him was a stack of true crime magazines.

"Been doing some studying?"

Reba Sue gave him a dirty look.

"Here comes your favorite part," Charles Lee said, looking at Susan with an amused smile. She smiled back at him.

Mr. Moose and Mr. Bunny Rabbit were setting up the scene for the ping pong ball drop on the Captain's head. Susan was on the edge of her little green padded chair waiting with anticipation, and down they came, bouncing off Captain's head. She giggled with delight, and then there was a loud "crack" over their heads. The ceiling opened up and one of the agents fell through, landing on Susan.

"Are you all right, Susan?" Charles Lee moved quickly toward her with his arms outstretched.

"Why are they here? Why was that man up above us?" Susan asked.

"I don't know. That was kinda funny though," he said, trying to make Susan stop whimpering.

At this point, Reba Sue came unglued. "You could have killed one of my kids!"

"I'm so sorry." Agent McGlinty laid on the floor next to Susan. He winced in pain. Reba Sue moved across the room and scooped Susan up, carried her to the couch and examined her leg.

"We'll need to take our man to the hospital. Will your daughter need to go, too?" asked French.

"Mr. French, I'm not leaving this house with you in it. Look what you've done to my home and my little girl. Just finish your damn search and get out," Reba Sue responded.

"What are they searching for, Mommy," asked Charles Lee. "Are they searching for money?"

She shot a look at him along with the other men in the room.

"Do you know where the money is, little fella?" asked French.

"I told you that I refused to speak to you without our attorney present and that goes for my son also. Don't you understand that law? I thought you guys were supposed to be smart."

"I am going to order you out of this house while we finish searching it. I was being nice to you, and now we are going to do things my way," said Agent French.

The sheriff went outside and explained to Charles what had happened. Charles was mad. Reba could hear Charles yelling at the sheriff.

Reba took the kids to Odessia's house and then went right back to her own home. She was not allowed back in, so she sat outside the house in her car, watching them. She didn't see them take anything out of the house. While she knew that there was nothing inside that would incriminate Charles, she was a little worried that they might find the hole under the burn barrel where they had kept the money before using it to bail Charles out last time, but they never even looked near it.

As soon as they left, she called Mr. King. She was afraid that her phone had been tapped, but at that moment she didn't care.

"Hello, Mr. King? You won't believe what just happened! They have arrested Charles for robbing a bank in Westville."

"Why in the world did they do that?"

"I believe that Miller and Black have given them false information in return for a lighter sentence. I'm sure that my phone is tapped."

"Yes, I could see that happening."

"They also searched our home and one of those FBI agents fell through my ceiling and landed on my daughter, hurting her!"

"Is she okay? Does she need to be seen by a doctor?"

"She is okay, but her leg is bruised. It scared her more than anything."

"Do you know where they took Charles?"

"He is at the Adair County Jail right now," she said, her voice beginning to quiver.

"Reba Sue, it's going to be all right. I'll see what I can do."

"They tore up my house. There is a big hole in my ceiling, and they have torn up my home," she cried.

"I'm sorry this happened to you and in the meantime just sit tight until I get back to you."

"Please don't say anything to Daddy. This is gonna kill my parents."

"I won't say a word about this, don't you worry."

"Thank you, Mr. King."

"Listen to me, Reba Sue, I think we need to bring in an old friend of mine by the name of Paul Hammer. I have spoken with Charles about this, but we need to move forward. Paul is a very sharp attorney who has a reputation for winning tough cases, and, like me, has good connections and knows the eastern Oklahoma US District Court systems and their judges. It will cost more, but it will be worth it, I promise you."

"I trust you to help us. If you say we need him, then hire him."

"I'll call him right now and see if he can get over to Stilwell this morning. He is a lot closer to you than I am, but if he can't come right away then I'll be there in four hours. Either way, one of us will be there soon."

"I'm going down there to find out what his bail is."

They said goodbye, and she hung up the phone, turning to look at her home. The agents had turned it upside down and she didn't know where to begin. She knew the feds hadn't found anything in this house. Anxious as she was, she was not worried about the search but rather about what those men had told the FBI.

Jeb Corey came and posted the bail for Charles. It was hard for Reba Sue to approach Jeb, but she did it anyway. In return for the bail, she told Jeb she would give him twenty head of her prime cattle as collateral, and as soon as the court hearing was over his money would be returned to him. Charles had known Jeb since he was a kid, since Jeb and Bud were close friends. They played and sang country and gospel music together, so he was like family to the Parrotts.

Jeb lived about a mile up the road from Reba Sue and Charles and would drive past their home each morning and evening. And it just so happened that he was one of the alibis that Rosey waved to on the morning of the Westville bank robbery. So, Jeb was confident that Charles was innocent and would not only put up his farm as surety for the bail money but would also testify on his behalf. Jeb told Reba Sue that she could keep her cattle because he had faith that Charles would be found innocent and his surety for bail would be returned.

Charles was released on bond and Reba Sue took him straight home. He took his clothes off and threw them at the wall, furious with himself for the mess he had caused. Reba Sue was running the bath water for him and letting him stew. She knew better than to start fussing with him about his big mouth and those boys from Wright City.

"Baby, I am sorry that I caused all this to happen," he said.

"Go wash that jailhouse off you," she replied.

He laid in the bathwater and soaked, thinking about how he would get out of this one. And the more he thought about it, the more he was sure that he would beat this case against him.

While he was soaking in the tub, the phone rang. Reba Sue didn't really want to talk to anyone, but the phone just kept ringing, so she answered it.

"Hello, Mrs. Parrott?" asked an unknown woman's voice.

"Yes, this is she."

"I need to speak with your husband. This is Lara from Mr. Hammer's office."

"He is busy right this moment. Can you call back in thirty minutes?"

"If you could just pass on the message that we urgently need him to come to our office in Muskogee. Mr. Hammer can see him tomorrow morning at ten o'clock."

"I'll tell him, and he will be there."

After his bath, Charles looked around the house, noticing where the FBI had torn the closet up and busted through the ceiling. They would never find anything here. He was not stupid. He called his friend Evan, who was a carpenter, to come and fix the ceiling.

The next morning, he drove over to Muskogee to meet with Mr. Hammer. Charles looked at all of the plaques and awards on his office walls. Looks like he's a very successful man, and it seemed that Mr. King was right to recommend him. His receptionist led Charles into Hammer's office. He was a tall, gray-haired man, who looked be the same age as Mr. King. After the introductions, Hammer got straight to business.

"We can speak openly. I want you to know that I'll do my best to get you out of this whether you're innocent or guilty. When we speak everything is confidential. So, tell me, are you guilty of robbing the Westville Peoples Bank?"

"Yes, I did rob the Westville Bank," Charles confessed, looking Hammer in the eyes to see if he flinched. He did not.

"Tell me about everything. Tell me what those Wright City boys know."

Charles told him everything. Hammer was impressed at the planning and detail that had gone into Charles's crimes.

"I have a solid alibi. Also, I don't believe that the bank president in Westville could really identify me. The banker stated that the man who robbed his bank was an older gentleman, and I am only twenty-six."

"Did you give the Wright City boys all the details of your disguise?"

"No, I don't think so. I was pretty drunk when I told them and so were they. I believe that they won't betray all my secrets."

"Don't be so sure of that," advised Hammer.

"I did tell them about another bank though," admitted Charles.

"Another bank?" Hammer asked, frowning and looking troubled.

"Yes, a bank in Vian. I robbed that one also. I'm hopeful that they won't give them that one too," said Charles.

"Let's just concentrate on Westville for now. If another comes up, we will go from there."

They spent the next hour establishing the alibi and where it took place. And there were two others that saw his impersonator that morning. It seemed that they had a good defense thanks to the multiple alibis.

"All right Charles, I'll request to question the boys from Wright City before the trial. The judge may or may not allow it, but we can at least try. Once I know more, I'll call you and set another appointment."

"I know we can win this. Are you going to tell Tom King what I told you? You know he's good friends with my wife's daddy."

"Charles, you need to know that Tom King brought me in on this case because he felt you would be more comfortable with me. That being said, he will know everything I know, you just won't be the one telling him, I will. We're good attorneys, and we will use every process possible to get you off this charge. We were both prosecuting attorneys for this court. You just stay out of trouble and let us handle the case.

For the next couple of weeks, Charles busied himself with his livestock and his family. He attended a few parties with Aunt Polly. He acted as though nothing had even happened, as if he didn't have a care in the world. The socialites of the little town seemed fascinated by it all. Everyone was talking about him.

He was out in the corral with his daughter, Susan, when a dark Ford Coupe pulled up to the house, and two men got out. One of them was Agent Golden. Moments later, the Adair County sheriff's car pulled up.

"Honey Girl," said Charles to his daughter, "go to your momma, and tell her we got company."

"Okay, Daddy." And off she went to the house.

Leaving the corral, Charles walked over to greet his uninvited guests.

"Hello there. What can I do for you?" said Charles.

"Charles, we have a warrant for your arrest for the robbery of the Vian State Bank in Vian, Oklahoma," said Golden.

"Really? Are you serious? Those Wright City boy have been telling you lies again, and you believe them? Are you going to tear my house up again?"

"We do have a search warrant, yes. I would like for your wife and kids to leave. I don't like scaring children, so please ask them to go now. We will conduct a search of your home and your property," announced Golden.

"We also have a warrant for your friend, Johnny Madden, aka Mad Dog," said Golden. "Can you tell us where we might find him?"

"No, I've not seen him in years."

"Charles, it looks like you have been very busy in the banking business," said Golden.

"I have no idea what you're talking about."

Reba Sue came out of the house, looking mad.

"Why are you here? I want you off my property unless you have a search warrant."

"I have an arrest warrant for your husband. I also have a search warrant for this property," said Golden.

She scanned the documents that he handed to her, this time crumpling them in her hand before passing them back and storming off back to the house.

"I'm getting my kids and leaving. I won't have you injuring my children again!"

"Thank you, ma'am," said Golden.

"Reba Sue, please call Mr. Hammer," said Charles.

"Where are you taking him?" Reba said to the agents, ignoring Charles.

"To Muskogee," said Golden.

Reba Sue got the children into her car and peeled out of the drive onto the dirt road. She was so upset she could hardly see straight. The kids were upset because she was driving so fast and fishtailing around a corner.

Charles Lee yelled, "Please slow down, Mommy! Please. I'm scared."

Tears were streaming down Reba Sue's face. She was furious. Where the hell was she supposed to go? Her parents lived hours away from Stilwell. She would go to Polly and Mom Parrott's house. She could not stand the thought of going over to Bud and Odessia's home. She and Odessia's relationship was becoming strained due to all of this.

She calmed down and took her foot off the gas, turning to check on the children.

"Mommy's sorry. I was mad, and I didn't realize how fast I was going."

"It's a good thing I realized you were going fast, Mommy," said Charles Lee.

"That is a good thing. I am so sorry, sweethearts. We are going to Mom Parrott and Aunt Polly's house for a little while. I bet Mom Parrott has a pie baked or some angel food cake."

"I love angel food cake!" cried Susan.

When they arrived at Aunt Polly's house, she was out in the rose garden cutting flowers with Mom Parrott.

"I want to help cut roses," said Susan.

"Of course, you can help, you're very good at picking out the prettiest ones," said Mom Parrott.

"Aunt Polly, could I please talk to you inside for a moment?" asked Reba Sue.

"Of course. Let's go inside."

Charles Lee started to follow them inside, but Polly stopped him, asking him to go and get the watering can and to water the roses.

Once they were inside the house, Reba Sue told her what was going on.

"Oh my God, Reba Sue! What can we do?" Polly said in a worried tone.

"I don't know, Aunt Polly. Those Wright City boys must be telling all kind of lies about him. I don't know what to do," Reba Sue sobbed.

"Oh, Reba Sue, this is real bad. I am so sorry this is happening to you and the kids."

"Polly, we may need more financial help with the bail. I hate to come to you and ask, but I don't know what to do," cried Reba Sue.

"I'll make a deal with you. If you can talk him into not robbing any more banks, I will get the money. But you have got to get through to him that this has to stop," Polly pleaded.

Reba felt somewhat relieved that Polly knew what was going on. She always knew that Charles's aunt had a heart of gold and loved her nephew and his family. She was always there for them.

"I will do my best Polly. This all started—"

"Stop! Don't tell me anything about it. The less I know the better. And who knows, the FBI could have my house and phone line bugged. You need to be very careful, Reba Sue. These agents will do anything to solve a case. They'll even lie and turn innocent words into guilty ones," she advised.

"Can the kids stay here until tonight?" asked Reba Sue.

"Honey, they can spend the night if you need them to. You know how much we love having the children here at the house. Call me and tell me the bond amount. I think I have enough left from the last bail out, but if I don't, we may need help."

"Can I use your phone? I need to call our lawyer," asked Reba Sue.

"Sure, you can. While you do that, I'll go get us a cold drink. I think I need a glass of Chardonnay. Have you told Odessia and Bud yet?"

"Oh no, I'm dreading it! But I'm gonna have to. That'll be my next call," Reba Sue started to cry again.

Polly handed Reba Sue a glass of Dr. Pepper and then poured a glass of wine for herself.

"Let me call them for you, Honey. You have enough on your plate right now."

"Thank you, Polly."

"Go on and make that call to the attorneys, and I'll go check on the kids."

"Thank you," said Reba Sue, turning and walking into Polly's bedroom to make the call.

Reba Sue called Mr. Hammer and told him what had happened. He reassured her he would go to the Muskogee jail and see what was going on. After the call she headed back to her house, arriving just as the feds were leaving.

She could see Charles in the back seat as the agents pulled out onto the road and drove away. She sat there and watched their dust on the dirt road settle, wondering if this was the end. Was he gone for good? The sheriff and two other men were finishing their search of the barn.

Reba Sue went inside to survey the damage. Yet again, the agents had made a terrible mess during their search. She started to cry and began picking things up.

Hammer put down the phone and shook his head. He was just heading out the door to spend some time with his wife Violet. They were taking a trip to Kansas City, and she was out in the car waiting for him because he had gone back inside to grab his gloves, which was when the phone rang.

"Honey, we are going to have to put off leaving for Kansas City. My client, Charles Parrott, just got arrested again for another bank robbery."

"How many banks is it now that he has been charged with?"

"Three, but I'm wondering if there will be more."

"He sounds like a professional criminal, Paul."

"Oh, Violet, you have to meet him. He is a fascinating character, clever and charming. I am not sure if I have ever met anyone like him."

"Now how long is this going to take? Maybe after you get things straight with Parrott, you and I can still go to Kansas City. I had my heart set on going to the Savoy."

"We will see, sweetheart. Let's go back inside and hopefully this won't take too long."

Hammer called the jail and asked Nelly Harper, the secretary, to call him when they brought Charles Parrott in.

On the trip to Muskogee, Golden tried to strike up conversation with Charles.

"Can I ask you a question?" said Golden.

"Sure, but that doesn't mean that I am going to answer it," grunted Charles, gazing out of the window at the bare winter landscape of Adair County.

"How do you have the balls to keep robbing so many banks?"

"I already told you that they are lying to you," he said.

"Charles you can make this a lot easier on yourself and your family if you just tell us the truth," said Golden.

"Go to hell," said Charles, "I'm tired of you trying to pin every unsolved bank robbery you have on me."

"Watch your language with me," warned Agent Golden.

Charles just shook his head and laid down in the back seat of the car. "I'm going to take a nap. I'm tired of your questioning."

There was silence. Charles lay there wondering just how much they knew.

When they arrived in Muskogee, they processed Charles through the jail, taking his wedding ring, watch, and wallet and putting them into a bag.

Hammer arrived quickly and went with Charles into a private room. As they entered, Hammer whispered to his client.

"Charles, be aware that we are most likely being listened to once inside this room."

Charles nodded his head to acknowledge Hammer's comment, and they sat down at the small table with two chairs.

"Charles, I am going to take care of everything. I just need for you to give me a list of places and people you saw on that morning that bank was robbed. I want you to think about what was going on that day. We are going to prove that these boys from Wright City are lying in order to get less time and less hard labor at Granite Penitentiary."

"Have they set my bond yet?"

"It's twenty-five thousand dollars. We will go before a grand jury on the charges in a month, so we have plenty of time to get our witnesses and alibis."

"How soon can I get out of here?"

"As soon as Reba Sue can get the money. And I'll call her as soon as I leave. Let's talk more once you're out," said Hammer.

"I'll sit tight."

Hammer walked out of there knowing that this was going to be a battle. Charles Parrott had robbed these banks, and if he could get him off the charges, then it would be a miracle.

After speaking with Hammer, Reba Sue called Aunt Polly to let her know the news. Polly said she could come up with part of the bail money, but that she would have to find someone to help with the rest.

Reba Sue called Dougal Knox, one of Charles older friends that owned a grocery store over in Greasy. Dougal and Charles had a long friendship, and she knew that he would help her if he could.

"Dougal, Charles has been arrested this morning for another bank robbery. I'm trying to get the bail money to get him out and we are short. Can you help me?" pleaded Reba Sue.

"Another one?"

"I know! It's like they are going to pin every unsolved bank robbery on him," replied Reba.

"I'll help you, don't worry."

"Thank you, Dougal! I'll make sure you get the money back. Polly and I are going over there in a few minutes to post her land as surety for the bail."

"I'll get my deeds together and go straight over there. They'll probably honor my land deeds for it," said Dougal.

"Thank you. I'll see you soon," said Reba Sue and she hung up the phone.

Once she had Charles alone, she would talk to him about changing his ways. Polly was right. He needed to get a real job and he needed to stop robbing banks. While it had been exciting and thrilling at first, now things were getting scary.

Polly pulled up and Reba Sue raced out the door to Polly's car, embarrassed at the disarray that her home was in.

"Dougal is heading over to help us pay the rest of the bail money, Polly," she said.

"Thank heavens for Dougal! I called Odessia and told her what was going on. She started having chest pains and dropped the phone, so Bud is taking her to the hospital. Lord, I hope she didn't have a heart attack, what with all the stress," moaned Polly.

"Oh Lord, I hope she's all right!" cried Reba Sue. Her head was spinning thinking about the stir this new piece of information would cause in the little town. Every time someone was admitted to the hospital it was in the newspaper. She could see it now: Odessia Parrott admitted to hospital on the day her son is arrested. Again!

"Let's go get this bail sorted, so I can get to the hospital," Polly said.

On the way there, they listened to big band music, Polly's favorite. Reba Sue hated that kind of music, but she tolerated it since it was better than talking about the mess that Charles was in.

Reba Sue led the way into the courthouse. She knew how things worked in a county courthouse, and so they approached the commissioner's office to provide the surety of bail for Charles's release. Once inside, a young lady asked how she could help them.

"We are here to pay a portion of Charles Parrott's bail," said Polly.

"I'll need your name and the deeds for property or the funds. Please have a seat, and I'll fill out the form."

The woman began typing out the surety information, all the while asking Polly questions. Polly had brought the deeds for all four rental properties she owned in town.

"You're quite the landlady," admired the woman.

"I am a businesswoman, young lady. I've been invested in real estate for a long time."

Polly was one of the most successful businesswomen in Adair County, and the fact that she was single and did it all on her own was all the more impressive. People also respected Polly for taking care of her mother, who had been the first female postmaster in Oklahoma. She, too, had done it all on her own, having been widowed at a young age and never remarried.

As the oldest child, Polly had picked up the workload when their father died suddenly at age thirty-two. Bud had been only seven and soon would become the man of the house. The Parrotts were a successful and ambitious family.

"Can we hurry this along? I need to get to the hospital," said Polly.

"Oh my, I'll type this up as fast as I can," said the girl.

After a few minutes, she had finished and had Polly sign the surety papers. She put down the pen and turned to leave with Reba Sue just as Dougal walked in.

"Oh, Dougal, this is such good timing!" said Reba Sue. "Polly has to get back to Stilwell immediately because Odessia has been rushed to the hospital. After you sign for the rest of Charles' bail, could you please bring him home? We have got to get back."

"Of course, I can. You ladies run along, and I'll take care of it."

Polly and Reba Sue hurried down the stairs, unable to get out of there fast enough. Polly didn't want to see Charles this way, behind bars or suffering the embarrassing ride home with Reba Sue. She was thankful that Dougal had arrived in the nick of time.

Dougal got out the deed to his farm and handed it to the young lady behind the desk. She started asking some questions and typing away.

"When can Charles leave?" enquired Dougal.

"As soon as the commissioner signs the papers, I'll call the jail and have him released. It shouldn't take too long."

Not long after that, the commissioner signed the documents and told the young secretary to call Agent French as soon as Dougal had left the office. French had asked to be notified as soon as Parrott was released.

Dougal went over to the jail to wait for Charles. He had told the jailer that he would be outside waiting, as it made him nervous to be in there. He lit a cigarette and was reaching into his truck for a drink of whisky when he saw a man in a suit approaching him. He decided to leave the whisky for later and walked toward the man and the door of the jail. The man kept walking and took a long look at his license plate as he passed Dougal's truck. Dougal noticed this and turned around to go back to the truck as if he had forgotten something. The man kept walking on down the block and went inside the courthouse. He was a fed; Dougal was sure of it.

Passing by the truck and entering the courthouse, Agent French wondered who that older man was. He looked too old to be a running buddy of Charles Parrott, so maybe he was an uncle. He would have to check him out, maybe follow them home.

Charles came out of the jail and strode up to Dougal with arms outreached.

"Dougal to the rescue," he called, slapping his friend on the back.

"Let's get out of here, Charlie. I think a G-Man just spotted me."

"Let's go."

A few miles down the road, Charles turned and saw the tail. He knew immediately that it was an agent and gave Dougal the heads up.

"Son of a bitch!"

"Hey, take the back roads Dougal over to Greasy. Let's see if he stays with us," suggested Charles.

Dougal did as he asked, and the agent stuck with them.

"When you get up over that hill pull under the bridge and take the fisherman's slot down to the river," said Charles.

They went up over the hill and quickly pulled down under the bridge. The tail kept on going.

"That was easy! Give me that whisky, Dougal. We need a drink."

They sat there for a while drinking and talking. Then they saw the agent go across the bridge in the opposite direction. They chuckled and sat there a while longer.

The next day, Charles went to see his mother at the hospital. She was mad at him and told him so in front of the nurse. He was embarrassed and ashamed of the pain he had caused her and Bud's family. He tried to reassure her that those boys from Wright City were lying but she was having none of it.

"You're just like your father!" she shouted. "You're a criminal, just like him."

Stung by his mother's words, Charles turned and left.

They came for him at six the next morning. He had slept in his bed for just one night, and then they had returned to arrest him again. He was going back to Muskogee jail. This made him furious, especially since this wasn't one of the banks he had robbed. They were arresting him for the robbery of a bank in Rush Springs, Oklahoma.

The banging on the door startled him. *Not again*, he thought, *surely this couldn't be happening again.* He hoped it was a dream, but the banging continued.

"Good morning, Charles," said French, smiling as the door opened. "I am placing you under arrest for the robbery of the First National Bank of Rush Springs."

"Could you not have done this two days ago, French? Or do you just enjoy putting the screws to my family?"

"You're the one who is putting the screws to your family, Parrott. I'm going to rid them of you and lock you up for committing these robberies."

"Go to hell, French!" shouted Charles.

Charles heard one of the children cry at the back of the house and decided that for their sake the best thing was to comply.

"Let's go. I don't want my kids to see this. Let me get dressed," sighed Charles.

"That suits me fine," said French.

Reba Sue never even got out of the bed. She knew when she heard the loud knocking that they were back for him. She just put the pillow over her head when Charles came into the bedroom and pretended to be asleep. He quietly dressed and went over and kissed her on the cheek.

"Honey, when you get up, please call Mr. Hammer and tell him I am at the Muskogee jail again. These bastards have accused me of robbing another bank."

"Charles," she murmured, "when is this going to stop?"

"I don't know. I don't know what to do."

She turned over letting out a low moan and began crying. He hated that she was so upset, but he knew that she would stand by him no matter what. She loved him or she wouldn't have put up with him this long. She knew that he drank and used drugs, which led to infidelities. He was a horrible husband and father, but they loved him. The kids and Reba Sue loved him, regardless of his nature. He would need to make it up to them after this was all over.

French didn't cuff him. They were beginning to get to know each other quite well, and the agent was confident that Charles wasn't the violent type. But then again, he could be wrong. This son of a bitch wasn't afraid to go into a bank with a sawed-off shotgun and threaten people's lives for money.

"French, my family and friends are running out of money for these bonds. This feels like you're punishing them."

"Hell, Charles, you could always go rob another bank and pay them back," said French.

Don't worry, Charles thought, *I plan on it.*

French took him to Muskogee, where the bail was set at five thousand. This lower amount was thanks to Hammer, who explained to the judge how hard this was becoming for Parrott's family. He assured the judge that Charles was not a flight risk and appealed to him for mercy. The judge considered this and dropped the bail from twenty-five thousand dollars to five thousand dollars, which Bud came over and paid.

When Charles was released to Bud a week later, his stepfather tore into him. He told Charles how Odessia blamed him for his part in the mess.

"Hell, she said it's because I bailed you out of jail the first time you got arrested for stealing those tires. She had wanted you to spend at least a week in jail back then, and I fought her on it. I thought it was no big deal, but maybe I was wrong. So, I let you sit in jail for a week this time, and hell this better be the last time, Charles. I don't have any more money or property to bail you out again."

"I hope this is the end of this Bud, I really do. These FBI are trying to hang every unsolved bank robbery that they have on me. But I'm going to get out of this. I have good lawyers. The best lawyers that money can buy."

"And who is going to pay them?" asked Bud.

"I am."

"Considering you can't even pay your own bail, I'm not even going to ask how you plan to do that," grunted Bud.

Charles had four pending bank robbery charges. Charles was antsy to get out and get money for the attorneys. He had been laying low and was keen to get around to robbing the Elkins bank again. He thought it would be easy to go back there, but he just wasn't sure when it was going to happen. Usually, Charles would wait for a sign, before he would go and rob a bank. That sign could be the weather, a bird or animal sighting or something that mysteriously told him it was time.

He'd gone over to Fayetteville, Arkansas to meet with his friend, Jess a couple of weeks earlier and there was a plan in place for the bank robbery. He would call Jess from someone else's phone on the day he would make a move on the Elkins bank. He still needed to figure out the alibi for the day of the robbery.

He was supposed to see Mr. Hammer again in a week so that they could discuss the witness list and other important details for the trial. It was going to be tough challenging the conspiracy charge in the Valliant robbery, but Hammer and King felt confident that they could have the bank robbery charge dropped. As for the charges of the Westville, Vian, and Rush Springs banks, they were working hard on those alibis and witnesses to the crime.

The FBI were definitely keeping tabs on him. He could hear them on the phone line clicking in, unless it was one of his neighbors. But usually if they wanted to use the party line they would chime in and say so. If he heard a click but no voice, he knew it was the feds. To test his theory, one day he purposely told a friend over the phone that he was going to look at some prime property the next morning. Sure enough, the next day there was a fed waiting outside down the road from the house.

Charles went back to the house and drank some more coffee. Sitting at the table, he came up with his master plan for the alibi on his own. He was leaving his wife out of this.

He promptly went out and got in his truck, driving twenty miles north to Tahlequah. He could see his tail in the rearview mirror. Entering the town, he drove past the Bank of Cherokee

County and slowed down, tapping his brake lights. Then he went down a side street and back around the bank. The tail was still with him. He turned and headed back toward Stilwell.

"I got a bite," said Charles out loud to himself. "Now I'm going to reel him in."

He turned up the radio and stepped on the gas, going a little over the speed limit. Then he got to the winding road down the mountain on Highway 62, and he pulled over into one of the lookout areas. The tail passed him, and Charles acted like he didn't notice. He just stood there a while, casually watching the fed drive down the twisting and turning highway to the bottom of the mountain. He chuckled and then got back in the car, driving off after the agent. When he reached the car, he stepped on the gas, passing the fed on the first straight away. He got a good look at the driver. He was a young-looking blond-haired man, Charles acted nonchalantly, just barely glancing at the agent, hoping that this young man would believe that he had no idea he was being tailed. He wanted the agent to be confident in his work that day.

Charles pulled into Mitch Murray's garage at lunchtime, finding the usual group of men hanging around. Mitch and Charles were very tight. He was perhaps one of Charles's best friends in Stilwell. Rosey's car was there, and Charles was pleased, as he was going to need Rosey's help with his alibi plan.

"Hey, fellas," Charles called out.

He was greeted with questions about his arrests, and he supplied some intriguing tales of the FBI and how Reba Sue had almost clobbered one of them for hurting Susan. There was a lot of storytelling, and the crowd of men were hanging on his every word. When lunchtime was over and a few of the men had gone back to work, Charles took Rosey aside.

"Rosey, I need you to be me tomorrow."

"No problem. What'cha need me to do?"

"I need for you to be here at Mitch's in the morning at around nine o'clock."

"I can do that."

"Then I am going to have you drive my truck up to Tahlequah. Maybe drive around the town a little. I want you to circle back around to the Cherokee County Bank and slowly drive by. There will be a fed following you most likely. Don't pay much attention to him. Just be cool and then take my truck back to my place and hang around a while. At one o'clock, head on back to Mitch's garage, tap the horn, and Mitch will open the garage door for you to pull in. Hang around for me, and we'll change back."

"That's no problem. I'll see you in the morning, Charlie."

"Thanks, Rosey," said Charles, turning to call to Mitch. "Hey, Mitch! I'm bringing my truck in tomorrow morning. Can I pull it inside the garage when I get there?"

"Sure, Charlie. But don't tell me why. I don't even want to know what you're up to," replied Mitch.

The next morning, Charles pulled into the garage, wearing his signature white cowboy shirt, aviator sunglasses, and cowboy hat.

"Morning, Mitch," he called out, getting out of the truck.

"Morning, Charles."

"I'm gonna change and have Rosey take my truck out of here. Let the feds follow him around for a little while," said Charles.

He pulled a suit out of the passenger's side out, grabbing a fedora hat and some nice oxford shoes. They were alone in the garage, and Charles undressed.

"If anyone asks, Mitch, tell them I came and asked you to fix a tire for me."

"All right, man."

Charles pulled out a sawed-off shotgun and some pillow-cases from the truck.

"Good luck today, Charlie. I hope you get what you need."

"I gotta get some money for the lawyer's fees. And if there is any leftover, you and me are going to build that race car we been talking about," Charles said.

Just then Rosey pulled up alongside the garage and came over, grinning from ear-to-ear.

"I think you got a fed out there waiting on ya," Rosey chuckled.

"Good," said Charles. "I need you to drive over to Tahlequah like we talked about. Then meet me back here around one o'clock."

"You got it," said Rosey and put on Charles's clothes, hat, and sunglasses. Then he started walking around the shop, imitating Charles's walk. Impersonating people was an art, and Rosey had Charles down perfectly. Charles laughed and so did Mitch, impressed at the likeness.

"Now hurry up, and get out of here before any customers show up," said Mitch.

As he pulled away in Charles's truck, they saw the blond-haired fed pull out of the car lot across the street.

"He took the bait," said Charles. "Can I borrow that Thun-derbird, Mitch?"

"I dunno, Charlie," Mitch said with a frown. "Why don't you take the Fairlane instead. It broke down in town the other day, and I've fixed it up for the owners. They're in Oklahoma City and won't be back to get it till next weekend."

"Great. That'll do."

"Just don't bring it back with any bullet holes in it. And if you get caught, I'm reporting it stolen," warned Mitch.

"I'll pay you rental on it."

"Now get out of here before someone sees you. When you come back, pull the car into the garage, and I'll get rid of any customers I may have."

Mitch went around and pulled the Fairlane into the garage. Charles slipped the gray suit on and tossed the gun, the pillowcases, and the hat onto the passenger's seat. He also put his change of clothes in the car and then slid behind the wheel. He put on a pair of dark glasses and backed out of the garage.

Before heading to the bank, he went to pick up Jess, his friend that lived in Fayetteville. They rodeoed together for a decade and Jess was up for the one hundred dollars Charles had offered him. He wanted Jess to drive him away from the Elkins area in the Fairlane. Jess was to sit at the same cemetery Charles had used before and wait for him. After the robbery, Charles would stop, change clothes and bury the loot and guns in the hole he'd dug weeks before. Then he'd return to the cemetery and leave the stolen car.

When he arrived in Fayetteville, he had Jess drive him over to the university where he found a 1953 Mercury that the keys had been left in it. He drove it away and Jess followed, and once they were at the cemetery, he transferred the gun, the pillowcases and the change of clothes to the car he had stolen and headed to the bank.

"This is a hold up!" he practiced. "I mean business!" He repeated this several times, puffing at his cigarette.

He knew this bank. The tellers had been very cooperative the first time just over a year ago, and the young teller had told Charles what times that time lock would open on the vault. It was straight up noon. The lock should be off. His heart was pounding as he pulled into the sleepy little town of Elkins. He drove right up to the front of the bank, he took a deep breath and pulled out the handkerchief he had brought with him to hide his face. Looking around and seeing that the coast was clear, he tied the linen around his face just under his eyes, then he pushed his hat down a little and grabbed the sawed-off shotgun and pillowcases. Another deep breath and he was out of the door making long strides toward the bank.

Bursting into the bank, all eyes fell on him.

"This is a hold up! I mean business!"

It was like a replay of when he was there before, except he was alone. All the same cashiers were there, and he put them to work, sending the same young lady to the vault. This time it was open. He hoped it would be enough to pay the attorneys.

JUSTICE FOR CHARLES

His bonds added up to over a hundred thousand dollars. His friends and his family were all standing by him. Even a county commissioner put up money and property for him. The Stilwell newspaper reported the four bank robbery charges against him, but most of the people in town supported him.

Here was why: He'd gone to a store last year on Christmas Eve and bought every toy and bike they had. The owner of the store kept this secret and also made out like a bandit. He loaded up trucks and went out to deliver toys to the less fortunate. Every Christmas day for the last three years, he took food, magazines, and cigarettes up the jail for all those guys spending the holiday locked up. He paid off a mortgage for a farmer down the road that was about to lose his place. He said he was paying his debts. Charles always wanted people to feel good and he had become a Robin Hood of sorts.

Reba Sue's family didn't put up a dime toward the rising costs of his bonds and attorney fees. They hoped that she would come to her senses and divorce him. His own mother, Odessia had struck a deal with Charles and Reba Sue. She would put up money, but they would deed the nice home over to her and Bud. The chicken house down the hill was finished and they would turn it into a home for Charles and Reba Sue. This way Odessia could watch over the kids since their parents had lost their minds. Reba Sue was furious but couldn't do a thing about it.

He had champion lawyers, and Charles believed that they could get him out of this. Hammer knew the system from the other side of the aisle as the U.S. District Attorney for the Eastern District Court in Muskogee, Oklahoma, from 1947-1957. It was the same court that Charles would be tried in. Charles liked how he could speak freely with Mr. Hammer, and he finally felt at ease with Mr. King. These two older men were tight. They'd served together in the Attorney General's office for the state of Oklahoma twenty years prior and they enjoyed working together on the challenge of getting Charles out of his legal problems. The court date for Valliant was set and they were ready.

When they got to court, Mr. King told Charles that his friend, Billy Black, had turned on him and that he would be the key witness for the prosecution. Charles was disappointed. He liked Billy and didn't think he would flip on him, but he also understood that he didn't want to do hard time in prison. No one did.

Billy Black took the stand and gave a detailed account on how Charles took them to a shop on the main street of Stilwell in the middle of the night and how he went into an upstairs attic in downtown Stilwell to retrieve a machine gun. He told the jury that the next day they traveled to Fort Smith, Arkansas, where Charles purchased bullets and a disguise for him to wear during the bank robbery. He told how Charles taught him to shoot the machine gun. And when he told the jury how Charles had driven through a church parking lot during the church service looking for keys in a car to steal for the getaway car, the jury all looked at Charles with disgust. Black went on to tell how Charles changed up his look and went to a used car lot and asked the man if he could test drive the car and then stole it for Black to use in the bank robbery. Black testified that he paid Charles a thousand dollars for his helping him and Miller to execute the robbery.

They didn't use Clark Miller to testify, only Black, since he seemed to be more believable and knew Charles better than Miller.

Later in the trial, the man from the dealership couldn't positively identify Charles. He was a master of foolery. The only person that the prosecutor had as their witness was Billy Black, a confessed bank robber. Hammer made sure the jury knew that Black had been offered a lighter sentence if he would testify against Charles.

On October 24, 1961, on the first charge of conspiracy to rob the Valiant Bank, the jury found Charles guilty and sentenced him to five years of prison and a fine of two thousand five hundred dollars. But the attorneys appealed the ruling, keeping Charles out of prison on bond. They had an ace in the hole. Hammer's secretary, who went to court on the first day to watch Hammer and King perform, noticed that the court reporter was not in attendance during the judge's instructions to the jury, and he mentioned it to Hammer. They kept this in their hip pocket, in case they needed to appeal. And they did need it. Hammer appealed the case, stating the instructions to the jury had not been recorded by the court reporter and that is not all that happened that day. Here's Hammer's secretary's, Clay Moore's statement:

> My employment for the past few years has been
> as secretary to the firm of Hammer and Atlas,
> Attorneys at Law in Muskogee, Oklahoma. The
> large amount of preparation in the many confer-
> ences preceding this particular trial had aroused
> my interest to a great extent. Also, some of my

friends had led me to believe that I was missing
an unforgettable experience, never having
watched Mr. King and Mr. Hammer in action
together in a courtroom. Since they were representing Charles Parrott the defendant, I asked
for and received permission of my employers
to go to court room when the trial opened.

Twelve people were called from the jury panel and seated
in the box. Judge Randall then stated to the jurors that this was
the case in which Charles Parrott was charged on two counts by
indictment, the first being conspiracy to rob a bank at Valliant,
Oklahoma and the second being the robbery of the bank.

Then the judge stated to the jury that the defendant was
also charged by indictment with robbing three other banks
in the Eastern District of Oklahoma. At that point both Mr.
Hammer and Mr. King were on their feet and Mr. King spoke
first, objecting to any mention of any other charges pending
against the defendant. Judge Randall told the attorney that he
was merely explaining to the jurors that they must not, under
any other circumstances, allow their knowledge of three other
cases pending to influence their decision in this particular case,
and that he it was really attempting to keep the atmosphere
clear for the defendant. Mr. King rose again and said something
to the effect that no amount of explanation now would undo
the harm that had been done to the defendant in mention-
ing the other pending cases. That it was entirely conceivable
several of the jurors did not know about those charges.

It was about that time that Judge Randall asked Mr. King
and Mr. Hammer to remain seated, and he would advise the
jury further as to their duties in arriving at a decision in this
case. He stated in effect, that there had been quite a bit of

publicity in the local news media and that any prior notions or ideas any member of the jury had conceived were to be entirely disregarded when deciding the case at hand. He then inquired of the jury if they felt they were able to make such a decision.

The defense attorneys again objected and asked for mistrial, but the judge overruled their motion, stating that he thought he was being entirely fair to the defendant, and he overruled the objections.

I remember looking around for the court reporter at that time, for I wondered how he was taking all of this down. Some of it was happening pretty fast, and I was curious to know if he, or she, was using shorthand, stenotype, a recording machine, or some dual combination of the three. I was never able to identify an official reporter.

After several questions to the original twelve persons chosen, having to do with any interest they might have had in banks, their personal acquaintance with the defendant or his family, any acquaintance with the defense attorneys or business with them, and several jurors were excused. I glanced at my watch and found that I should have been back at the office long before. I left reluctantly, hoping to return after the jury had been chosen so that I could at least hear the opening statements, but I was never able to get back to courtroom during the trial.

*   *   *

This ensured an appeal if they needed it, and they won his case four years later on April 20, 1964, with a mistrial. The FBI were furious that he'd gotten off on a legal detail. During that time, while out on bond, Charles robbed other banks in the small towns of Taylor and Atkins in Arkansas and another one in Advance, Missouri. And he did it all while the FBI were watching him closely. He was ecstatic that the attorneys had won this case.

When the FBI had arrested him on the Rush Springs bank robbery case, he was pissed because didn't rob that one. This case went on for over a year. The attorney for the Eastern District Court made a motion to drop the charges on April 30, 1962, after the arrest of the man that actually committed and confessed to the robbery.

In the Westville case, the trial lasted for three days, and Billy Black's testimony did not convince the jurors of his guilt. Charles had left Slim's hat in the getaway car, and the hairs in the black hat left in the getaway car didn't match Charles's hair because the hairs belonged to blond-haired Slim. The FBI couldn't come up with those yellow cowboy boots that the bank president said he could identify if he saw them. There were many alibis and witnesses stating Charles couldn't have been in the Westville area. One of them being Emma Jean Hankins who was at the bank that morning and then saw Rosey whom she believed to be Charles as she passed the Parrott place on her way home. The other alibi witness was Jeb Covey who had driven by the Parrott place also and he had helped pay his bond since he believed in his innocence. Charles and Reba Sue's brilliant manipulation of his whereabouts was very well planned, and it paid off. He was acquitted.

Charles came up with a crazy plan for his defense on the Vian bank robbery and he called Slim and asked to meet with him over at Dougal's place. They had a plan, and it was a good one. The only catch was, that Slim could become tangled up in this mess.

The next morning, Slim went to go over to Dougal's place. Bud, the attorney, Paul Hammer, and Charles were there waiting for him. Dougal got on the phone and called his friend, E.W. Floyd, the sheriff of Sequoyah County, and told him to go over to the Vian bank around noon and he would see something very interesting. He and E.W. had been friends for a long time. Dougal didn't like fooling with his friend, but he did it for Charles.

Charles gave Slim a set of his clothes, the signature black cowboy shirt, Wrangler jeans, cowboy belt with a big shiny buckle, green felt cowboy hat, and the aviator sunglasses. Bud, Mr. Hammer, and Slim got in the car and headed over to Vian. It was a short twenty-minute drive, and Slim was nervous as hell. When they pulled up in front of the bank, Mr. Hammer told Slim to just do as they had rehearsed, and everything would be over in a matter of minutes. Slim nodded and took a deep breath.

As they walked into the bank, Bud nodded toward E.W. Floyd, the Sequoyah County sheriff, who was leaning against the back wall of the bank. E.W. was Charles "Pretty Boy" Floyd's brother, and he definitely took a different course in life than his brother. E.W. nodded back toward Bud.

The bank vice president, Mr. Westfield turned, saw them and looked alarmed. He knew Bud Parrott and just assumed that Slim was Bud's son. Of course, he knew that Charles Parrott had been indicted in this robbery.

Mr. Hammer addressed Mr. Westfield, introducing himself and saying that they needed to see where the crime was committed.

Mr. Westfield points at Slim and says, "What'd you bring him for?"

"He wanted to see it too," says Hammer.

"I'll tell you one goddamn thing, he's seen it before," stated the vice president of the bank.

Now, Slim had never been to Vian in his life, and so you know that tickled the shit out of Mr. Hammer.

Slim approached the teller's booth and asked for change for a twenty. He lifted his hat off his head, showing his wavy blond hair and looked at her over the rims of his glasses. The teller, Ms. Stuffle, bolted to the back of the room and asked another teller to wait on him. She was terrified. A younger lady came to the booth and made change for his twenty and they left the bank.

As they got into the car to leave, Bud told Slim that he did good. Slim asked if this could get him arrested and Mr. Hammer told him that all he did was ride along to see the crime scene and that was all there was to it.

Three weeks later the court date arrived. Slim was told to take the first seat he could find in the courtroom and not to start any conversations with anyone. Mr. Hammer cross-examined the bank vice president, Mr. Westfield, and asked him if he remembered identifying the man that he brought into the bank three weeks ago. He replied yes, and he remembered that day very well. Mr. Hammer asked to approach the bench. Once the judge had heard what he had to say and saw that E.W. Floyd was in the room and could be called on to testify to clarify this information the district attorney requested to dismiss the case.

Charles had beat each conviction. Most people would have stopped at this point. But the game between the FBI agents and Charles had just begun. Charles loved to trick 'em and fool 'em. And he loved robbing banks.

The chicken house home.

Reba Sue despised living there. The outside looked aw-
ful, but the inside was filled with expensive décor.

THE SUBMARINE GETAWAY

After Slim had helped with the court case. The FBI paid him a visit. French knew that they were good friends and now he was going to press Slim on that relationship with him.

Agent French went to Slim's house, and he wasn't alone. He had the bank president from Gracemont with him, the man that that Charles had shot. Now that really cracked his nerves, but he stayed steady as he could, and he tried to change his voice and accent. He had done a lot of talking in that bank and he wished he had kept his mouth shut. What if that man recognized his voice?

"How long have you known Charles Parrott?" asked French.

"Since I was thirteen," he replied.

"That's a long time. Would you say you're one of his best friends?"

"We don't live in the same town, and I don't really see him very often anymore."

"You went with his father into the Vian Bank, didn't you?" French asked.

"Yeah, I did. I am friends with his father, Bud, and he asked me if I wanted to go along, so I did. I had dropped into Stilwell to see Charles, and he wasn't home, so I went by his dad's place to see if he was there. That's when Bud asked me if I wanted to ride along to see the bank in Vian," said Slim.

"Did you rob the bank with him in Gracemont?" Asked French.

"No, sir, I did not."

"Do you recognize this man? The man he shot that day?"

"Agent French, I am not aware that he robbed any bank in Gracemont or anywhere for that matter. I believe he was acquitted on those charges and as long as I've known him and his family, he has always been respectful and law abiding."

"I'm going to be watching you. I have a feeling you know more than you're admitting to," said French.

"Fine by me. I don't know why you would want to watch me, but if you want to you certainly can."

Then the agent went and paid a visit to Slim's mother, and that was it. He couldn't rob another bank with him now that the FBI were involved. They weren't a secret anymore, and Charles was being watched, and he was still robbing banks. It scared the shit out of Slim. He was out. When he told Charles of his decision, it was understood, and they didn't see each other for a while. Charles would find someone else to help him.

Charles had several groups of friends. There were the bootleggers, the guys from the racetrack, and then there were the cowboys. The Stilwell cowboys were the ones he was closest to, and it wouldn't take him long to find another accomplice.

Aunt Polly and his mother, Odessia, wanted Charles to get a job. This bank robbing business had almost killed Odessia. She had a two heart attacks during those four years of court battles. And even though he was acquitted later, the effects of his behavior were taking a toll on his family. And he needed a real job. He couldn't go around acting like he was some champion cowboy. His few wins through the rodeo season weren't enough money to provide for his wife and two kids. Reba Sue was the bread winner, and the Parrott women wanted that to change. Polly called Rusty Weaver and asked him to give Charles a job on his construction crew, and he agreed.

Little did Polly know that he would be meeting one of his best bank-robbing partners at his new job.

Cotton Wainright was a smart, good-looking kid with blond hair and a small frame. He knew about engines and building things. He'd been working for Weaver for a couple of years and was one of his best workers. Now sometimes Charles would work, but not that often. One day they were working over in Farmington, Arkansas, and he borrowed Weaver's truck and took young Cotton with him. Charles said that they'd be back shortly, and they left Weaver out there and didn't come back. He was mad and ready to put a dent in their heads. He had to hitchhike home and when he arrived his truck was sitting there in the driveway. Ends up, they went and robbed a bank. To cool him off about stranding him out there, Charles shows up at Weaver's house later that night with a big sack of money and lets his kids, all four of 'em, reach into that sack a pull out as much money as they could. One of them got four hundred dollars. Then he let his wife grab a handful too. Charlie Weaver forgave him after that night. Hell, everyone in his family loved Charles now.

That was the beginning of a three-year partnership with Cotton beginning in 1962. Cotton was dedicated and loyal to him. Charles liked how quiet Cotton was and how well he followed direction. They call themselves "The Minute Men." Getting in and out of the bank within five minutes was their mission.

Charles decided on the next bank. They would cross the border to Arkansas and rob the Hindsville Bank. It was a small town and had no police station. Cotton came up with a getaway idea that Charles loved. They called it the "submarine." Cotton had an old washer and dryer that he hollowed out. They would load them onto a trailer, along with some furniture and look as if someone was moving. Rosey would be the driver of the truck pulling the trailer with Cotton and Charles hiding inside the washer and dryer.

The morning was quite cold, and Reba Sue had bundled up Susan and Charles Lee to stand on the road and wait for the school bus. The children were eight and ten years old, and she worried that the kids at school might say something about their father being a bank robber since the whole town knew what he did, but those kids never said anything about their dad.

Reba Sue was waiting for Tommy Porter to show up to take her to work. Tommy would be Charles's decoy alibi. Cotton has already come and picked up Charles before dawn to head to Arkansas with Rosey, driving the truck and trailer. When Tommy arrived, Reba Sue gave him the white shirt, sunglasses and Charles's cowboy hat to wear.

"You're a dead ringer for Charles," said Reba Sue.

"I'll take that as a compliment," replied Tommy.

They got in Charles's truck and headed into Stilwell to the courthouse where she worked.

"I have a good idea. When we get to courthouse, we need to make sure someone sees you drop me off, so we will sit in the truck until we see someone. Once we do you can pull out to leave me, and I'll yell at you, and you pretend you don't hear me and drive away. That will establish a better alibi with a witness seeing you drop me off," said Reba Sue.

"Brilliant idea."

"Here's the clipboard and paper to write down the names of people you see on the streets of Stilwell. It's very important that you write down a time and location of anyone you see."

"Got it."

When he pulled up, it was perfect timing. There were plenty of people arriving for work at the courthouse. He leaned over a gave her a peck on the cheek and Reba Sue laughed and hopped out.

She walked a few steps and turned to yell at him as he was pulling away. "Charles! Charles!" she called to him.

Missy Howard, her coworker was walking up, and Reba Sue spoke to her.

"I know he heard me," said Reba Sue.

Missy just shook her head, and they walked into the building together.

Tommy knew his mission would pay well. All he had to do was drive around for a little while and keep his mouth shut.

Tommy drove around town and then headed back to the Parrott place, where he changed back into his clothes and left the clipboard on the table. Tommy's wife was waiting there to pick him up when he arrived.

"Mission accomplished?" she asked.

"Yup. I just hope him, Cotton, and Rosey make it back home," Tommy replied.

"I have a feeling that they will," she said with a smile.

Meanwhile, Charles had Rosey sit on the side of the road on Highway 45 three miles west from the bank. When they passed him, he would follow them to a dirt road that led to an old cemetery, and there the guys would hide inside the washer and dryer on the trailer. And for the first time in a long time, Charles would take the money with them on the trailer. He had confidence in the submarine getaway.

Cotton had stolen a brown 1960 brown Chevy in Missouri to drive to the bank. Charles was no longer taking chances on taking an employee's car. They were dressed in Army coveralls that Rosey's wife had found for them and they used handkerchiefs for their masks.

When they arrived, there was only one man inside the bank.

"We want your money," Charles told the banker.

"There it is. Help yourself," said the banker.

Cotton ran over and started taking the money out of the cash drawers and loading the pillowcase while Charles pushed the banker into the vault and told him he wanted all the money.

"You've got it all," he said.

Charles shoved the man into the vault and slammed the door. They jumped in the Chevy and headed west out of town. They went roaring by Rosey and pulled into the cemetery. Cotton was trying to get out of the coveralls and noticed that Rosey wasn't following them.

"Charles, I think he's asleep in the truck," said Cotton.

They had gotten up at five in the morning to drive over, and Rosey must have fallen asleep while he waited on them.

"How the hell does anyone fall asleep while we're doing a bank robbery? Go down to the road and get his ass," said Charles

Cotton was scared to go back down to the road, but he did it and sure enough Rosey was asleep. Cotton laid on the horn, cussing Rosey under his breath. Rosey about jumped out of his skin and put the truck in gear following Cotton.

"I'm sorry, Charles. I was so damn tired," said Rosey sheepishly.

"Goddamn it, Rosey. Are you trying to get us caught?" Charles asked.

Cotton climbed into the dryer and Charles climbed into the washing machine with the pillowcase full of money. Rosey had messed this one up. They had left the coveralls and hat on the ground there at the cemetery in their haste to get out of there.

Once on the highway, Charles would peek out the top of the washer to see. Later he said he felt like he was in a submarine raising the telescope to see what was going on. Charles saw a roadblock ahead and lowered the lid, being very quiet.

Rosey slowed to a halt and an officer came up to the window of the truck.

"What's going on officer?" asked Rosey.

"The bank in Hindsville was just robbed. Have you seen two men in a brown Chevy on the road?" He asked.

"No, sir. I haven't but I haven't been on the road long," Rosey replied. "Just taking some junk over to the dump."

The officer looked at the trailer but didn't investigate it as cars were piling up behind Rosey. He waved Rosey on through.

When they made it to Stilwell, Rosey pulled the trailer onto his property and Charles and Cotton climbed out of their hiding places. Charles handed him a couple hundred dollars and told Cotton he would count the rest and give him his cut later in the week. Cotton left in his car and Charles unhooked the trailer and took Rosey truck over to his Aunt Polly's house, where he buried the money under a large oak tree, then he returned the truck to Rosey's place and Rosey gave him a ride home.

"I'm sorry I fell asleep, Charles," Rosey said.

"You could have really screwed us up on that one. I gotta be able to count on you, Rosey. How the hell do you fall asleep during a bank robbery getaway?"

"Y'all are having all the fun and my job is boring is how."

"Don't you ever do that again," Charles said in a mean voice.

Rosey knew he might be out of the crew for this one.

A couple of days later the story of the robbery was in the newspaper. As Charles read it, his face flushed. The article said that there were three hundred dollars in the coveralls left at the scene with the stolen car. Had Cotton robbed the bank robber?

COUNTING BULLETS

I 'm going to kill him this time," said Reba Sue as she swung the car onto the highway. Her new Mercury had plenty of get up, and Charles Lee, and Susan flew across the seat into the door. They had seen Charles coming down the highway and had swiveled their heads, watching him go by with a woman sitting close to him. He had always cheated on her with other women, but recently he was being downright blatant about it.

Reba Sue accelerated and struggled to bend over her large, pregnant belly. She reached for the gun, that was always under the seat and when she came up with the large Colt pistol, Charles Lee and Susan crawled over the seat and into the back floor of the car.

Susan looked over the seat at her, tears are streaming down her reddened face as she cusses under her breath. This was the first time Susan had heard her cuss. She had a bad temper and mixing in the pregnancy and bruising of her ego was making this situation far more dangerous.

She rolled down the window and leveled the heavy pistol, firing off two shots. The cold February wind blasting into the car with the smell of the gunpowder mixed in with it.

Susan began to cry quietly, as Charles Lee counted the bullets.

"She's got four bullets left," Charles Lee whispered to Susan, wrinkling his nose.

The kids had seen a lot in their young lives, but they had never seen their mother fire a gun at their father. Being raised by Charles and Reba Sue wasn't easy, but they had dealt with it the best that they could. They were eleven and nine now and beginning to see that their parents were far from normal.

The car swung off the highway onto a dirt road and Charles Lee got his courage up and raised his head to see what was going on. He dropped right back down onto the floorboard.

"He's pulling over," he whispered to Susan with a worried look.

"Momma, please don't kill Daddy," Susan whimpered.

She got no response. Their mother acted as if they weren't even there. She got out of the car with the pistol. Charles Lee and Susan raised their heads to watch the carnage that was about start. Charles started walking toward her, and she fired a shot, striking just a yard or so from his feet. He hardly flinched.

The girl sitting in the truck swung around in her seat at the sound of the gunshot. She was wearing his cowboy hat, and she quickly removed it and slid down in the seat.

"That's three bullets, and she's got three left," Charles Lee said.

"Now, Reba Sue, please. This is Leland's little sister, and I'm just taking her home," he pleaded. "Please don't upset yourself over this. I promise you Reba. That's what's happening here."

"Charles Parrott, you're a liar, I saw how close she was sitting next to you. Tell your whore to get out of the truck."

"Honey, please," he begged. "The kids are in the car."

She said nothing and fired another bullet into the rear tire of the truck.

"What's a whore?" Susan asked Charles Lee.

Charles Lee just shrugged his shoulders and said, "I'll ask around later."

Charles went to the truck and told the young brunette to get out. After she slid out of the truck, Reba Sue yelled, "Put his hat back on."

Charles reached in the truck, got the hat, and gave it to her. She slowly lifted it onto her head. The poor girl wished she had never fell under his spell. He guided the girl around to the back of the truck where Reba Sue waited for them.

"There you go. You look real cute in that hat. How old are you? Nineteen, twenty maybe?" Reba Sue asked. "To young to be riding around with a thirty-two-year-old married man."

"Mrs. Parrott, I was just getting a ride home from your husband. I had no intentions of doing anything with him," she said.

"I oughta shoot that hat right off of your pretty little head for lying to me," Reba Sue said, turning the pistol toward the girl.

The girl peed her pants.

"I thought only kids did that," Susan whispered as she watched.

Charles Lee shook his head with a smirk.

Charles started toward Reba Sue, and she turned the gun back on him. Charles knew how to manipulate bad situations; he was good at that.

"Take the hat off, throw it on the ground, and stomp on it," Reba Sue ordered the girl.

Charles intervened, "Baby don't make her do that. I paid a lot of money for that hat."

The girl did as she was told not even waiting to hear Reba Sue's response to his plea.

"You need to calm down," he raised his voice.

"Go to hell," she screamed.

Susan launched her body halfway out the window and cried, "Momma, please don't shoot Daddy. Please, Momma, you and Daddy get in the car and let's go home."

The girl looked at Susan like she was a superhero, who'd come to save her.

"Go get in the car with the kids," Reba Sue said. "We're leaving this whore on the side of the road where you probably found her."

Charles and the kids sat in the car not saying a word because they were glued to watching Reba Sue give the girl a lecture. When Reba Sue came back to the car, she came to the driver's side and told Charles to get in the passenger's side. As he got out of the car, she hit him across the back of his head with the barrel of the gun. He yelped but didn't raise his hand or voice toward her.

"Don't you ever embarrass me again with this shit. I'm sick of it. You said we were starting over. You said you'd stop robbing banks and running around on me."

Charles barely had a leg in the door when she floored the car, fishtailing on the dirt road, throwing dirt and rocks against his truck and the girl.

The ride home was silent. As soon as they arrived, Charles got on the phone with Rosey and asked him to go get his truck and the girl. As soon as he hung up, Reba Sue tore into him. He was sitting at the dining table. When she told him that he was becoming nothing but a drug addict and a drunk, he threw a saltshaker at her. The shaker hit her pregnant belly. She winced and started crying in pain. He jumped to comfort her and apologized profusely, telling her that he would make things right.

The next day Charles went to see his old friend, Odie Nofire. Charles respected the older Cherokee and always went to him for advice. They would drink, smoke marijuana and have deep conversations about life and how to live it. Nofire told him he needed to save his marriage and move far away from Stilwell as soon as the baby came. Nofire had very good intuition and he told him that the FBI were going to catch him if he didn't leave Stilwell. He told Charles that an opportunity would present itself soon to travel far away.

ALASKA

On February 1, 1966, Charles robbed another bank. He liked to rob banks when there was bad weather in the forecast. The headline that day was:

TWO ROB HARTFORD BANK AND FLEE ON SLIPPERY ROADS

This was the only bank he would rob in 1966. He was under a microscope, being watched by the FBI day and night. He set up another decoy to pretend to be him. Tommy Porter obliged and spent the night at the Parrott house. In the morning he put on Charles's signature look and started off by driving Reba Sue to work and waved at the FBI men that sat down the road. Charles watched as the FBI pulled away to follow Tommy and Reba Sue. Nothing like having the FBI as your alibi.

Cotton came to the house, and they got ready to go. He knew that Charles would question him about the last robbery and how the newspaper had said there was money left in a pocket of the coveralls he wore.

"Cotton, you know I trust you, but I want to know why the newspaper reported on our last robbery, that there was a couple hundred in the pockets of your coveralls," said Charles.

"Charlie, I wasn't stealing money from you. Maybe those people was trying to create strife between us," said Cotton. "Maybe the FBI did that, because they know we are a good team."

"We are a damn good team, and you always follow the plan, Cotton. And even if you did that. I forgive you, because I can always count on you to do a good job, and this time we are gonna switch things up."

"What you mean?" asked Cotton.

Charles pulled out a lady's dress, coat and black hat, some stockings and lady's shoes. He had taken these from Aunt Polly's house, mainly because she had big feet. He hoped they would fit Cotton.

"You want me to wear that?" Cotton asked.

"Yup. You're going to make a real pretty woman," he said with a smirk.

Cotton put on the outfit and looked in the mirror. "Oh my God, I do look like a woman."

"Your legs are too hairy but pull on those stockings and see if those shoes fit," said Charles.

Cotton did as he was told, and the shoes fit although they were tight. "I ain't putting on any makeup. This is as far as I'm going on this deal."

"Come on you gotta put something on your eyes," said Charles as he rummaged through Reba Sue's makeup. "Here is some eye shadow. Now shut your eyes and I'll put it on you."

Cotton grimaced and let him apply the makeup.

"Damn, Cotton, you look pretty. I can't wait to see if they think you're a woman."

What an odd-looking pair they were. On the drive over, the snow was falling pretty heavily, and the roads were becoming very slick. This time Cotton asked for everyone's car keys at Charles's request. He didn't want anyone following them ever again. Once they cleaned out the tills and the vault, Charles went back in the lobby area, and he herded everyone into the vault.

Once outside of the bank they drove slowly on the slick roads to a strip mine to dump the stolen car and get in with a young native girl that Charles had recruited. It went off like clockwork and he wouldn't rob another bank for over a year.

French was mad when the agent tailing Parrott told him that there was no way that he could have robbed that bank, since he had him in his sight all morning. French told him to stay on him and to let him know if the snitch they had in their pocket had anything to say about it.

He went to his office to write his report on Parrott. FBI Director, J Edgar Hoover had requested that French write a custom detailed report on Parrott. He wanted to know more about him.

```
PHYSICAL DESCRIPTION OF CHARLES
HARTWELL PARROTT
Race          White
Birth         10/19/34
Height        6'
Weight        165
Hair          Dark brown, no trace of gray
Eyes          Hazel
Complexion    Tan
Build         Slender
FBI No.       536 384 D
Characteristics  Very Polite


PERSONAL HABITS AND PECULIARITIES
Wears Levis and western clothes, including
cowboy boots, constantly

Has been known to enjoy drag racing and
motorcycle racing. He has owned a drag
```

racer and race motorcycle and attends
drag meets.

PLACES OF AMUSEMENT OR HANG OUTS
66 Service station in Stilwell, Oklahoma

Rodeo events where he participates in
Bronc and Bull riding.

LEGITIMATE ACTIVITIES
Subject generally works in the Stilwell,
Oklahoma area, tending livestock.

However, he has been employed as a rodeo
performer and judge of bucking partic-
ipants.   He has been employed as a
shooting gallery concession operator
and gun fighter at an Oklahoma City
amusement park.

FAMILY
He is married to Reba Sue Parrott, maiden
name Snow. They were married right after
graduation of high school and have
known each other since age fifteen. She
currently works at the Adair County courthouse in the welfare department and has
worked for the McCurtain County and the
Oklahoma County as a typist since she
graduated high school.

They have two children, Charles Lee age
eleven and Susan age nine.

RESIDENCE
Parrott lives five miles south of
Stilwell, Oklahoma. His residence is
peculiar in that Charles's parents live
in a nice brick home, and he and his

family live down the hill from them in what looks like a chicken house. Once inside the chicken house, I found that it is filled with expensive furniture and appealing décor. He is trying to look like a poor man.

French wrote a detailed report about how many associates he had and the vehicles he had access to. There were a total of twenty-six men and women that French considered part of the Parrott gang. There were many rodeo riders, cowboys, cowgirls, natives, childhood friends, and bootleggers on the list. His list of vehicles is longer than his list of associates.

In wrapping up the report, he states that he was indicted for four bank robberies but had beat all the charges. He also believed that Parrott has robbed at least seven banks in the past four years.

March 1966

Reba Sue was very hormonal during her pregnancy, and Charles took the brunt of it. Reba Sue wasn't going to cool down until Charles started acting right. She'd heard the rumors of the young native girl he was running with, and then there was the incident with the kids and the bullets flying.

Charles knew that things had to change and that he didn't want to lose his wife and kids. In addition to robbing banks and philandering with other women, he knew that he had to get a handle on his drinking and the pills.

Reba Sue had given him an ultimatum and demanded that he quit drinking after shooting at him and scaring the girl in his truck. She wanted him to understand that she did love him, but she would not live with a husband that cheated on her. With the arrival of baby Toni Lynne, he started trying to be a better man.

They had been living in Stilwell for six years now, and Reba Sue was sick of the small-town gossip that swirled around Charles and their marriage. She wanted a change, and boy was she getting one. Charles had convinced her that Alaska would be a fresh start for them. He would quit robbing banks and try to make it up to her.

His good friend from Broken Bow, Wiley McGillis, had moved there a year ago and encouraged Charles to come up there. There were good jobs and very few women.

When Toni Lynne was only three weeks old, Charles left for Alaska, going ahead of his family to secure a job and a place for them to live. He joined a union so he could work as a longshoreman. He was optimistic, and he wrote Reba Sue a long letter telling her how much he missed her and needed to see little Toni Lynne. He told her to pack up and fly out there. He also told her to contact Hunter Nofire and he would help her with her finances. He'd found an apartment in Anchorage, Alaska, and he'd gotten furniture, linens, and things for the kitchen. He wanted his family there and he was ready for their new life to begin.

Charles Lee and Susan were upset that they were leaving their relatives, their horses, toys, and pets. Everything would be left behind. They each had one suitcase to pack all their clothes in. No toys … nothing.

Reba Sue was exhausted a lot of the time. Susan tried to help with little Toni Lynne as much as she could. Reba Sue was losing her mind trying to prepare to move to this place so far from home, but she was hopeful.

The day Odessia took them to the airport in Tulsa, Susan clung to her, crying uncontrollably. The kids wouldn't have her or their Aunt Polly there. Charles Lee was stronger; he didn't cry once.

Odessia took Susan's face and kissed her on each cheek, whispering, "Don't worry, Honey Girl, you'll be back soon. I just know it. Your momma isn't going to like it there, and I bet you come back before winter comes."

Charles Lee was excited about flying. Susan was to upset to be excited about that. All she could do was hold onto to her grandma's handkerchief she'd given her and smell the White Shoulders cologne that still lingered on it.

Reba Sue struggled with the baby on the plane. When little Toni Lynne finally settled down and fell asleep, she leaned her head against Susan and said, "We just gotta make it there, and everything will be fine."

As they flew over the Gulf of Alaska near Anchorage, the view was beautiful. They had never seen anything like it.

The new home in Anchorage was an apartment, and they were on the top floor. Reba Sue seemed to approve of it. As soon as Charles Lee and Susan got unpacked, they headed downstairs to check things out.

They found some kids that lived in their building and made friends. Susan's new friend, Lindsey, age ten, was from Texas, and she cussed a lot and bragged about how everything was better in Texas. She was annoying, but Susan needed a friend. These kids were from all over the United States. Their families had come to Alaska for work. They didn't meet one kid who was from the area.

Charles Lee and Susan continued to scout the new surroundings. After a while, they noticed that all the other kids had been called inside for the evening. Charles came out and told them that they needed to get inside. It was almost ten o'clock. They couldn't believe it was still light outside.

None of them could sleep that night with the sunlight coming into their bedrooms. Reba Sue went out the next day to buy heavy curtains, hoping that would help them sleep. Then she went to the grocery store where fresh vegetables and fruit were scarce. It seemed that those items came in a can here. She wasn't happy when she couldn't find any tabasco sauce or Dr Pepper. When she got home, she immediately got on the phone with her mother and asked her to please ship her some tabasco. She told her mother that it was like they had moved to another planet.

That evening Susan saw her new friend, Lindsey.

"Where the hell were you today? I was excited that I would get to introduce you to everyone at school," said Lindsey.

"It's summer, and we just got out of school for summer break," Susan responded.

"We go to school during the summer here. You better tell your dumbass parents to get you in school."

"Hey, don't you call my parents dumb."

"I'll call 'em whatever I want to."

Susan slugged her in the stomach, and Lindsey ran away crying. Susan went and admitted to her mother what she had done, and they waited for Lindsey's parents to show up at their door, but they never did.

The next day, Reba Sue took the kids to their new school and got them enrolled. Susan was in Lindsey's class, and she was shocked when recess came, and Lindsey introduced her to everyone, telling them that Susan was her new best friend.

After about a week at the new school, an alarm went off. Susan and Charles Lee didn't know what was going on. Everyone crawled under their desk. Their teachers explained that this is an earthquake drill and then told them of the destruction of the big earthquake and tsunami of 1964. They told their mother about it and Reba Sue worried about living on the top floor of the big apartment building. They eventually had a mild earthquake, but it was enough to rattle the china in the cupboard. Reba Sue rushed the kids down four flights of stairs and outside of the building. It was early in the morning, and they were all in pajamas, not knowing what to do. Reba Sue was developing a hatred for Alaska. This wasn't going to last.

Charles started committing petty crimes to make easy money. He quit his job as a longshoreman and began stealing copper and selling it to his friend, who owned a salvage yard. Then he started drinking again, and Reba Sue wasn't going to put up with that. Their dream of starting over was falling apart. They were fighting a lot, and one night he broke the glass shower door with his fist during an argument. They both started crying and talking about moving back home. They had only been in Alaska for two months.

That week, Charles got a U-Haul and loaded everything up. Susan said goodbye to Lindsey, who had taught her how to play spin the bottle with a bunch of young boys and girls. Charles Lee's new friends had taught him how to graffiti a building with a four-letter word that he didn't even know the meaning of. Charles Lee liked Alaska and wondered why the heck they were leaving. It was a hectic time for the family.

Driving through Canada was beautiful, but slow goings since it had started snowing. When they finally arrived at the United States border, the patrol would not allow Charles to take the U-Haul trailer across the border because he had no papers for it. The fact was he had stolen the trailer. Now he took the trailer down to an area with a lake and he took the back seat out of the Mercedes Benz and started loading things in there. There was just enough room for Charles Lee and Susan to sit in a hollowed-out area. Reba Sue was furious with him.

On the long drive home, they stopped off at Yellowstone Park. The bears came up to the line of cars moving slowly through the park, and they were finally having a little fun on this hellish trip. They fed the bears bread through the window of the car.

That was the best day of the trip and it looked like Reba Sue was loving him again. She was laughing and laying her head on his shoulder. Maybe things were going to be okay.

Working as a longshoreman in Alaska

Charles and Susan

THE HAT ON THE BED

Agent French had informed the Alaska Bureau on his move, and they had nothing to report. They said he was working on ships as a longshoreman, and it seemed he'd gone straight. He and Agent McGlinty met to discuss how they would handle Parrott, now that he was back in Oklahoma.

"He'll be back at it," said French.

"I'm not so sure. Maybe he's trying to appease his wife. From what I hear from my informant in Stilwell, the move was to save the marriage," said McGlinty.

"If the marriage fails, I believe he will rob more banks. I think he enjoys it a bit too much and the son of bitch is good at it," replied French.

"The whole damn town of Stilwell alibies him every time a bank is robbed. Even my informant is tighter lipped about him these days. Sometimes I wonder whose side they're on. Last time I talked with one of his neighbors who had been contacting me regularly, she said she didn't want to work with us anymore. And she was my best informant. She listened in on the phone's party line for information and had given me good information for over a year. I hate losing her, because I can't get anyone in that town to work with me, except the town drunk and I think he's just taking my money and lying to me. There is an older Cherokee man that Charles spends a lot of time with. His name is Hunter Nofire and he's known to have strong connections to the Chief of the Cherokee Nation. Charles is in constant contact with Nofire and has been for years. I've tried to talk with him, but he won't cooperate at all. I tried having Nofire tailed and he vanishes in to thin air. Charles goes to his home up in the hills and doesn't come out for days. I'd like to know what that is all about."

"Good luck on Nofire. I'm going to pay Charles a welcome home visit. Feel him out a little," said French.

French called and set a time for the meeting. He didn't want to just show up. He wanted to make a connection with Parrott, and he didn't want it cut short because he surprised him. Maybe Parrott would slip up. When he called him, he was surprised at how he welcomed him to come over. This was going to be interesting.

Charles was in the garage working on a motorcycle when he arrived.

"That's a nice Triumph you have there," said French.

"I used to race motorcycles when I lived in Oklahoma City. You ever hear of a guy named Gary Nixon? He's a flat track champion, and he won his first race on one of my bikes when he was just a kid. Sometimes I wish I had kept racing cars and motorcycles. You got any hobbies, French?" Charles asked.

"I don't have a lot of time for hobbies. I'm not home much, and that's unfortunate because I would love to have a motor-cycle," said French, trying to connect with him.

"So, what brings you to visit with me?" asked Charles.

"Now that you're back in Oklahoma I wanted to ask you if I could call you if we have a bank robbery, so I can verify your whereabouts. What would you think about that?"

"I wouldn't mind. But what if I'm not home? Are you going to accuse me of robbing it? This seems kinda tricky. I can't see it working very well, but you're welcome to give me a call. I'm not a bank robber, but if you choose to believe those Valiant boys so be it. They are out of jail now, maybe you should be calling them when a bank is robbed."

"All right, well, that is what I wanted to talk to you about. What are you doing for work right now? And how are your wife and kids?"

"Reba Sue hates your guts and thinks you have ruined our lives. I'm working for a friend by the name of Manuel Hightower, building chicken houses. Please don't go harassing him and his family. I'm lucky to have a job with him. You guys have damn near ruined my reputation in this town. My parents and aunt have had their names tarnished also and that really makes me mad. You guys go around questioning my friends and their families, and you scare them and make accusations. It's not right what you do to my friends and family. I've learned that the FBI will do whatever the hell they want to whether a person is guilty or innocent," said Charles. He was getting more and more angry.

Agent French knew he was wearing out his welcome. He had wanted to establish a working relationship with him, but he could see that wasn't going to happen.

"I'm sorry about that, Charles, but it's part of my job. I won't bother your employer."

"Thank you. I need my job. I've got to get going now. Do you have any other questions?"

"No, that's it. Thank you for speaking with me and agreeing to my calling you whenever a bank is robbed."

Charles pulled the motorcycle out of the garage, revving it as French started his car and pulled out of the drive. French was going down Highway 59 toward Stilwell when Charles flew around him on double yellow lines going about a hundred miles per hour. French smiled at this and thought, *this guy runs on adrenaline. He's a bank robber. He's got it in his blood.* French had seen it before in other criminals: a thirst for speed and excitement.

The visit just fueled Charles to go rob a bank. He would get back to his house in warp speed and wait for French to call. This would be a fun challenge for him. He called Rosey and asked him if he wanted in. The planning began, and he wanted to do it quickly. He picked up Rosey and began the hunt for the next bank. It would be Hubert, Oklahoma, a town that was thirty-five miles from Stilwell. They set the plan in action.

This time the alibies were set with the usual decoy, Tommy. The wife of one of his friends made him and Rosey grocery store aprons and they wore them to rob the bank. They had little white paper hats, sunglasses and handkerchiefs. When they entered the bank, Charles took his voice to a higher tone to try and make it seem that they were younger. And he only spoke twice during the robbery. They got ten thousand dollars out of the bank and made it home in twenty-five minutes. Just as he walked in the door the phone rang. It was French. He grabbed the alibi clipboard to see who his alibi was.

"Charles, I'm just checking in on you. We had another robbery," stated French.

"I'm home, and I've been home all morning. I have someone who drove by my place when I was out feeding cows and I waved to 'em. You could call 'em and verify if you want. It was Mr. Wayne Rogers who lives down the road from me."

French thought he was lying. He knew that Charles could drive fast, and there was no doubt in his mind that Charles had robbed the bank. It had only been a week since they had met. He knew Charles enjoyed this.

Charles and Reba Sue's marriage was falling apart. He wouldn't come home for days at a time and when he was home, he'd be tipsy from drinking and taking pills.

At the Adair County Fair, Susan was singing with her class on the main stage. She and her classmates wore white cowboy shirts, wheat-colored Wranglers and white straw hats. That day, she had gotten dressed and was really excited about the evening.

Charles came into her room and saw that her white straw cowboy hat was on the bed! Susan panicked and grabbed the hat, setting it up on the dresser.

"I saw that!" Charles exclaimed.

"I'm sorry, Daddy. I don't know how that happened," Susan said. Tears welled up in her eyes.

"It's okay, sweetheart. Although you may have cast some bad luck for tonight. Mom Parrott may not win the pie contest at the fair." He chuckled and gave her a hug.

Charles had so many superstitions that it was hard for Susan to keep up with all of them, but this one: Never put a hat on the bed! That was a bad one. Someone was going to get hurt or something really bad might happen.

Charles was very intuitive. He needs the planets to align whenever he's doing something important.

There's was a horseshoe over the entry to their home. The horseshoe must be hung above a doorway with the ends facing up so that good luck doesn't run out. The horseshoe is considered a repellent of bad spirits, because of its crescent shape that resembles a new moon. This crescent shape is feared by the "little people" a.k.a. goblins. Susan was terrified when he told her that story and Charles Lee thought it was hilarious.

Charles also thought that boots were good luck. He would nail one to a fence post to keep good luck over the herd. And when he rode a bronc or bull, he always wore one pants leg tucked in his boot and one out for luck.

And then there was salt. Salt is believed to be a talisman or a good luck charm. Charles taught the kids to toss it over their shoulder and put a pinch in their pockets to protect them. Add in a rabbit's foot and you're fully protected to have a good day.

If there was a black cat crossing the road, they weren't going that way. His kids didn't know why he was like this, but it sure kept things interesting.

Charles was excited about the fair. He was showing Reba Sue's beautiful sorrel colored thoroughbred, Beech-nut in the horse show. The horse had won several races and horse shows. He was Reba Sue's pride and joy. Mom Parrott had entered her famous apple pie in the baking contest. It was going to be an exciting evening at the fair.

After school, the kids went over to the fairgrounds. Susan's group of fourth and fifth graders actually sounded good when they performed their three songs. Of course, they started off with "Oklahoma," then did "Hello Dolly," and ended with *The Sound of Music* song, "Do-Re-Mi".

After the performance, Reba Sue and Charles took the kids to eat fair food. Charles Lee could eat a million corn dogs. Baby, Toni Lynne, who was now a year and a half old was fascinated with a balloon tied to her little arm.

After dinner, Charles Lee went with his friends to see the coon dog contest. Reba Sue, Susan, and Toni Lynne went to check on Mom Parrott's apple pie entry. Charles wandered off with Rosey, telling Reba Sue he would catch up with them at home and that he had to make sure her horse was taken care of.

Mom Parrott was waiting patiently as the judges tasted the pies. She had brought hand churned vanilla ice cream to go with her apple pie. Her à la mode serving made a good impression on the judges and they placed the blue ribbon next to her pie plate. She was thrilled and told Susan that she would make sure to teach her how to bake the perfect apple pie, but that Susan couldn't give away her secret recipe.

It had been a fun night until they saw Charles drinking in the parking lot with Rosey. Reba Sue got the kids in the car and pulled up to where they were hanging out beside the horse trailer.

"Charles, are you coming home soon?"

"Yeah, I'll be there soon. Don't worry about me," he responded.

"All right," she said and pulled away saying something under her breath.

Charles didn't come home that night or the next night. He didn't call either. Susan told her mother about that hat the bed and that he might be injured somewhere.

He finally came home three days later, without her horse. He told her some stupid lie that she didn't believe regarding his whereabouts and told her that he had sold her horse to a man from Colorado. She told him to go get her horse back and he said he couldn't even remember the man's name. Then he went to bed to sleep off whatever he had be on.

She went out to his truck where she went through the ashtray, finding cigarettes with lipstick on them. Then she found a pill bottle. Those bottles were starting to appear more frequently. She started crying, and then she went inside and started packing suitcases. He woke up and tried to calm her down, telling her it wouldn't happen again, but she knew it would.

Reba Sue got on the phone with her mother and told her she wanted to leave Charles. They wouldn't be a family anymore. It was over.

When Reba Sue arrived at her parent's house in Golden, they were welcomed with long hugs and reassured that everything was going to be all right. Her parents had moved out of their nice bedroom to the sleeping porch, giving the kids their bedroom. Charles Lee, Toni Lynne, and Susan would share the bed, and Reba Sue would sleep in the other bedroom. Their lives changed that day and sleep would not come for any of them that night, except for baby Toni Lynne, who lay beside Susan, smiling in her sleep.

Beech-Nut

Charles showed up a couple of weeks later with a Honda 50 for Charles Lee and Susan. Charles said they had to share it, but Charles Lee definitely took ownership and Susan let him, since her father told her he was bringing her a beautiful paint pony he had his eye on.

Susan and Charles Lee thought maybe their parents were going to get back together, because their mother was being nice to him, but that was not what this meeting was about. Later in the day, they would end up at the courthouse, where she had filed for divorce. Once they had signed papers and were outside on the courthouse lawn, they had a short conversation.

"Reba Sue, I'm going to move down here and date all the pretty girls in McCurtain County," he said.

"Go ahead and see if I care. You've been doing that for a while now. You'll end up in jail pretty soon without me to keep you safe," she responded.

"You're probably right," he said and walked away.

After that day men lined up to go on a date with Reba Sue. She was as popular now as she had been fourteen years before. There was also a man that she worked with in Stilwell that drove down to Golden to take her out. His name was Roy Keen, and he would take her and the kids on their dates, unlike her other suitors.

She got a job in Idabel working at the courthouse. The same place she had worked when she had graduated high school. She was happy again, and she had her confidence back. She was a new woman, and Charles wasn't liking it one bit.

Once Charles moved back, he was quickly reunited with all of his old friends. He was looking for a new partner, and he found one in Jonesy Monson. Jonesy was a tall, good-looking, dark-haired cowboy with a bit of a criminal past. They had known each other for a while. One night he had a long talk with Jonesy. He was working on reeling him in, which wasn't hard.

"Jonesy, I think we'd make good partners. Let me just tell you a little bit about bank robbing," said Charles.

"Tell me about how you do it," Jonesy replied.

"I go and I look at the bank, and I figure out if I can rob it or not. When you're robbing banks, you may look at thirty to find one. I mean, when you got so many to look at, you make it like it's a vacation. You drive all over the country and just look and look and look. The main thing you do is you stay up late at night studying maps and seeing the population of towns, and you know the ones you want to look at because it's twenty miles from the county seat and it's gotta have at least two or three roads leaving the area. It's gotta have a good hiding place because you have to change cars in five minutes after you leave the bank. You have to become this other person by changing your appearance also. You figure how long it takes them to phone the police and how long for them to get there. Also, you figure how long it would take them to throw up the roadblocks."

"Okay and what about the actual robbery? What goes on inside the bank?" asked Jonesy.

"What you do is you tell yourself, 'I'm going to own this bank. This is going to be my bank for a while. I'll own, it and everyone will be working for me.' I used to go in and get the money myself, but the longer you go, the smarter you get, and you figure out the lady that handles the money all day can sack money ten times faster than I can. You might leave money that you don't know about, but she does."

"How do you keep cool once you're inside. I might lose my wits once I walked in the door," asked Jonesy.

"You will be fine."

"Do you have one lined up now?" asked Jonesy.

"Yeah, I do. I've been studying up on a bank in Dierks. They have a large amount of money for payroll for the lumber mill every two weeks. If we time it right, it will be a big payout. Are you interested?" he asked.

"Yeah, I am. When do you want to rob it?"

"Next week on Friday morning. I need to get some alibies and a decoy for me. We need a stolen car to drive there, and I already have a change out spot where we change clothes and the vehicle. Come over on Thursday night, and we will go over the details. I think we will be good partners, but you can't tell anyone about us or what we're doing. Swear to me you will keep this quiet."

"I swear I will, Charlie. I want some of that money. What's my split?" Jonesy asked.

"Fifty split."

"Okay, I'm in."

Dierks was forty miles away from Broken Bow, where Charles now lived. He would have liked a shorter distance, but this could be a big take. He didn't care if French called him. He had a good solid alibi set.

That morning, Jonesy was nervous, but everything went off like clockwork. They wore oversized white shirts and large white Mexican cowboy hats that Charles had bought while in Mexico a month earlier. The large wide brims made for an odd look, and Charles loved it. Jonesy was stone cold quiet during the robbery, watching Charles in action. They were in and out in less than five minutes. It was over almost as soon as it had begun.

Jonesy was impressed. They stopped on the side of a dirt road, and Charles jumped out and took the guns and money and dropped them into a hole he'd previously dug. He didn't worry about Jonesy coming back and taking the money, as he would never find it and only Charles knew about the marker he had left earlier, which was a fence post with a white mark that was barely noticeable that he had painted earlier. As they drove on, he tossed the hats and large white shirts out of the car as they crossed a river bridge. Once they were at the abandoned barn where they had hidden an old truck belonging to a friend of Charles, they changed into their cowboy clothes and headed back to Broken Bow.

"Jonesy if you keep your mouth shut for the next couple of weeks, we will go back to the hidey hole and collect the money. You'll know how much is in there when you read the newspaper about the robbery and how much was taken. So, don't worry that I'll cheat you. That would be stupid. What I need for you to do is not to talk about this to anyone and I'll give you your half. Understood?" asked Charles.

"Yeah, I got it. That was easy and I want in on the next one."

"We have to be cool for a while, and then there will be a next one. Right now, just be cool. Don't talk about it to anyone. Just know that the FBI agents are keeping an eye on me. Half of the time they follow me around. After I go into a café or a shop, they ask to see the money I paid with, looking for marked bills. Just know that if you and I are friends, they'll come around to you ... don't talk too much to 'em. Keep everything very vague. Tell 'em that you and I are nothing but rodeo buddies."

French called Agent Golden after he got the news of the bank robbery in Southeast Oklahoma. Golden had recently been moved to that district.

"Charles Parrott is at it again. Now he's back in McCurtain County, and the wife has divorced him. My gut tells me he is going to go on a run of robberies. Nothing stopping him from being reckless. Get some good informants on him."

"I'm already on it," said Golden.

PATSY

When Charles laid eyes on Patsy at the rodeo, he was awestruck. She was petite with long brown hair, and she wore beautiful western clothes. She had a way about her that drew him in. He wanted to meet her, and he asked Jonesy to set it up for him. Jonesy had known her for a long time and obliged Charles.

Jonesy asked Patsy to meet him one afternoon at the Broken Bow Café and said Charles would be there also. He assured her it was just a friendly get together.

"He just wants to meet you. Nothing else," said Jonesy.

"I remember seeing him when I was a sophomore in high school. He was always with Don Delow. My girlfriends and I would envy them in their fast cars, and they were always slicked up."

"He hasn't changed much since then," said Jonesy with a grin.

"But why would he want to meet me?"

"I'm not real sure, but he just asked me to introduce you," said Jonesy.

They had been waiting a while for Charles to arrive, and Patsy was about to leave when he walked in.

He came through the door of the café and when they locked eyes, she didn't know what happened … he had her mesmerized. She tried to put her guard up with him, but she didn't stand a chance.

"Good evening, Patsy. I'm so glad you came to have dinner with us. I've been watching you compete at the rodeo, and I think you're very good and I must admit. I find you attractive."

She blushed and lowered her head, raising her eyes to meet his, and it was all over. He reached over and touched her hand. Electricity ran through her, and there was no doubt in her mind that they would be together. After that evening, they started dating, they would be inseparable and devoted to one another. He could be himself with her. She knew coming into the relationship what he did and what he had done in the past.

Patsy had two young children, Robyn and Ricky. Charles made sure they knew he loved them also. His kids were a little older, but they all got along well. Moving to McCurtain County had worked out for him. He was close to his kids, and he had a new wife who was more suited for him. Even Reba Sue liked Patsy, and this helped Charles to better communicate with Reba Sue, which wasn't an easy task. Things were going better than he could have ever imagined.

Then the Lockesburg bank robbery happened, and he did something he shouldn't have done.

He was hanging out with his old friends in Broken Bow, and he began plotting to rob a bank in Lockesburg, Arkansas, with Sam Sargent. Sargent was an older man with a long criminal past. He was also the uncle of Jonesy Monson and had taught Monson a lot about stealing cars and all kinds of petty crime.

The two young sons of Wiley McGillis, Brody and Russell talked Charles into letting them be involved. The boys had grown up knowing Charles. Brody was nineteen and Russell was twenty-one and if Wiley had known what Charles was about to get his boys into, he would have killed him.

Charles was schooling them on how to rob a bank. They drove the routes with him to the bank and to the getaway spot where they would change their clothes and they stole a car in DeQueen, Arkansas, to use for the robbery. They had planned everything out, but when the day came to execute the robbery, Russell McGillis had said something to Charles that he didn't take well, and he was upset with Russell. Charles went and robbed the bank by himself earlier than the planned time, that morning.

He thought the young men wouldn't try to rob the bank without him, but they were on their way to commit the robbery when they were arrested. They had no idea that Charles had already robbed the bank and the police had been alerted.

FOUR HELD IN LOCKESBURG BANK ROBBERY

Sherriff Louie Hilton of Sevier County said today $12,000 to $13,000 was taken Wednesday in the robbery of the Bank of Lockesburg.

Hilton also said he was continuing to hold three men and the wife of one of them, all from Oklahoma, for questioning in the robbery. One man and the woman were being held at the Polk County jail and the other two were transferred to Nashville.

Hilton said a lone gunman walked into the bank, forced bank employees to lie on the floor and ordered the bank president and his wife to clean out the vault and cash drawers.

He said the man was wearing coveralls and had a woman's stocking over his head.

The sheriff said the man is believed to have escaped in a stolen car, possibly one that was stolen Tuesday at DeQueen. He said however that another stolen car from Paris, Texas found in the area could be the getaway car.

The sheriff said while on his way to the bank to investigate the robbery, he had stopped to question a woman when he saw her parked on the side of the road. While he was talking to her another car pulled up. It was Marshall Graves, publisher for the Nashville newspaper. Then a truck pulled out from a side road and made a U-turn and fled at a high rate of speed. He handed Graves one of his pistols and told him to take the woman to Lockesburg. Then the sheriff took off in pursuit of the truck with the three men inside. The sheriff cornered them at a dead end after firing several shots, they surrendered. He found two .38 caliber revolvers and changes of clothes in the truck.

They would be tried and found guilty. Charles was sickened by it. He'd given Wiley five hundred dollars right after their arrest to hire a lawyer for his sons, but Wiley let the public defender represent them and the daughter-in-law. The public defender did a horrible job. The jury deliberated for less than one hour and recommended fifteen years for the men and five years for Russell McGillis's wife, Ruthie. She was only nineteen.

Sam Sargent was also arrested and charged with conspiracy to rob a bank. He was sentenced to ten years in prison.

None of them ratted on Charles, and they were all sent to Cummins Prison in Arkansas.

He had robbed three banks in a matter of nine months. He himself said to Reba Sue that he had gone berserk after the divorce. He did love Patsy, but he would still confide in Reba Sue about what was going on in his life. They still had a connection and always would. When he told her about the three banks, she was angry with him.

"What the heck do you think you're doing, Charles?" Reba Sue asked.

"I don't know. I've kind of lost myself, lost control of what I'm doing."

"You're going to be arrested if you don't cool it. Then how will I take care of the kids? What will Patsy do? You can't ruin her life too."

"Did I ruin your life?" he asked her.

"Yeah, you did. And now everyone in McCurtain County knows what you did to the McGillis boys and that poor young girl. You ruined their lives, too. When are you going to stop robbing banks and ruining the lives of others?"

"I'm going to leave here. I'm taking Patsy and her kids and moving back to Stilwell. I can't stay here. I think I might buy Dougal's store and try the straight life. Promise me that the kids can come to Stilwell with me every now and then. They're going to be upset that I'm moving away."

"If you can go straight, that'll be a miracle. I'm all for it, but I know you, Charles, and I know you won't stop. I don't think you can. Just don't endanger our kids or I'll kill you myself."

"Does that mean they can come to visit?"

"Yeah. It's Christmas break next week, and I'll let you take them if you like."

"Toni Lynne can go too?"

"No, she's just a baby. She should stay with me."

"She's never going to get to know me if you never let her come with us."

"Let's not argue about this. She shouldn't go. She's too little, and besides Susan needs time with you right now. Toni Lynne won't remember you moving away, but it's going to break Susan's heart."

He would take the kids with him to Stilwell for Christmas. When he told them he was moving, they were shocked. They thought everything was going well and didn't understand why he had to move. Then he told them it was because he was buying Dougal's store. This seemed to smooth things over with them. He said there would be many train rides for them to take to see him, and they loved riding the train, so that softened the blow.

Just after Christmas, he took Patsy and her children to visit his mother's family in Blue, Oklahoma. His cousin, Donald was home on leave from a tour in Vietnam and Charles wanted to see him.

They arrived during a snowstorm. Everyone had a good time visiting, and Donald told them some stories about the war. He had been issued a new uniform and duffle bag, and Charles asked if he could try on the old uniform. It fit him and Charles asked if he could have it. Donald gave both the bag and uniform to him. He didn't know why Charles wanted it, but he gave it to him.

The next day after the roads had cleared up just enough to be drivable, Donald wanted to drive into Durant. He hadn't been home for a couple of years, and he wanted to see as many folks as he could during his leave. Charlie got in the car with him and his daddy. Patsy said she was going to drive into town in a little while, and Charles told her to pick him up on the town square. They were visiting with lots of folks on the square, and Charles was strolling around the square, seemingly separating himself from Donald and his father, Ed. Then Patsy pulled into a spot on the square. He went over and told Donald and Ed that he would see them back at the house.

As Donald and Ed continued walking around the square, they saw Charles milling around, looking inside cars. They saw him slip into a car and pull out with Patsy following him in her car. They both knew that he was a bank robber, and they couldn't believe what they'd just seen.

That day Charles robbed the Bokchito Bank after he left the town square. The bank was just five miles from his grandparent's place, and Charles, Patsy and the children were back at the house before Donald and his father, Ed returned."

He and Patsy were giddy and in good spirits that afternoon. When the news came on that evening, they all learned that the bank had been robbed, Donald and his father exchanged troubled looks. Charles just looked at them and grinned.

Donald, Ed, and Charles had been watching the nightly news and had heard about a search for an escaped convict in the area. Then, they learned that the bank robber had told the bank president he had been in prison for eighteen years, and all he wanted was the money. When the anchorman said that the getaway car was found a half mile from the bank and that it was stolen that morning in Durant they knew, without a doubt, they were sitting there with the bank robber.

Charles had taken the money and hid it in a hollowed-out trunk of a pecan tree in the large orchard behind his grandparents' home. They came back a couple of weeks later and got the bills out of it, but he'd left the silver inside the tree. He had a plan for those coins.

In the spring, he took Patsy's kids out to the field with a wagon and told them there was buried treasure. As they ran around looking, he would tell them if they were hot or cold, and when little Ricky found it in the tree, his eyes lit up and they put as much silver in the wagon as it would hold. He was like a leprechaun leading them to the pot of gold.

Patsy Beck with her daughter Robyn.

HARTFORD

Agent McGlinty, the FBI agent that had been on Charles's trail for the past eight years, came to see Charles.

"I'm retiring, and this is my last week. I tried to get you every way that I could, but if I couldn't get you fair and square, I didn't want you. But I'm telling you there's one coming to take my place and he won't play like I did. His name's Harry Folger, and if he thinks you're guilty, he'll see to it that you're guilty," said McGlinty.

McGlinty shook Charles's hand and left. The conversation had been short and to the point. McGlinty was telling him to cool it, saying that the new agent would be dirty and giving him a warning. Charles couldn't believe the agent had come to him with this information, but he took it as a challenge. A new player had entered the game and Charles wanted to prove he could outsmart him.

McGlinty was right. Folger was as dirty as they came. He told Charles right to his face that he was going to nail him, any way that he could. Charles thought that Folger might even have him killed.

Patsy felt fear in her heart. She knew Charles felt that fear too. He got to where he didn't want to tell her when he was going to rob a bank because she would cry and worry. What scared her the most was that the FBI were coming for him and waiting for him to trip up. They knew that they were being followed and watched closely. Charles coached her and her children in talking to the FBI. One day when the FBI were questioning Patsy at the front door about his whereabouts and he was hiding in the bedroom, he prompted Robyn to go to the front door and say," Momma, when is Charles coming back from his cousin's house?" Of course, they believed the child and turned to leave.

Charles and Patsy were running Dougal's store and living out at Lake Tenkiller State Park in a cabin while looking for a home in Stilwell. It was hard for Patsy to run the store. She had no experience at being a shopkeeper, and it was exhausting. Patsy had made friends with Tommy's wife, Anna, and that was a comfort to her. She and Anna would practice barrel racing together. The two couples became very close and spent a lot of time together.

Charles's family were happy he'd returned to Stilwell with his new wife and her children. Odessia and Polly hoped he had changed his ways, but Bud knew Charles was most likely still robbing banks. Bud was right.

February 15, 1968

Charles had his alibies set. He would drop in to see Liza Carol. He and Liza had been friends for a long time. They had agreed that he would come to the shop she owned on Main Street, and she would confirm that he had come in several times during the day. Then he would also see some town folks that morning that he could count on for an alibi for him. After that, Rosey would pick him up and sneak him out of Stilwell, and they would head to Hartford, Arkansas, to rob the bank.

Rosey had been a good partner in the past, and Charles figured they would get back to it. It had only been one month since he robbed the Bokchito bank and the game with the FBI had intensified and he was ready to outsmart Agent Folger.

Charles was arrested that afternoon. A state trooper pulled him over south of Stilwell in his new 1968 maroon Javelin sports car with no license plate.

He was taken to the jail in Stilwell where he was held overnight, saying they have to confirm that the car wasn't stolen. The next morning, he pled guilty to the charges of no license plate and a defective muffler. He paid the fines that added up to sixty-three dollars. He thought he was going to be released, but he was told there would be a hearing date for a fugitive from justice charge, and it would be held at the county courthouse in Stilwell. Arkansas had started extradition proceedings to return him to Arkansas for the holdup of the Hartford Bank. He would need to post a five thousand dollars bond and go to trial.

When they had arrested him and put him in jail, they found a receipt in his wallet with the name Joe Longshore. This name was one of his aliases. Things were unraveling for Charles.

Aunt Polly called one of her best friends, Bessie Miles. She knew that her grandson, Sam Miles was an attorney in Arkansas. Bessie put her in touch with him.

Sam had just started practicing law and felt he wasn't equipped to handle a case of this magnitude, and from what he'd heard, the authorities were really committed to getting him behind bars. When he met with Polly, Odessia, and Bud, Charles's mother made the remark that he looked a little young to be taking on the case. He was a tall, handsome young man, looking to be younger than Charles. Polly defended Sam Miles. She wanted to hear what he had to say.

Sam had thought this through, and he had a plan. He was working with a good trial lawyer by the name of Mac Dover. Dover was a white-haired, old Southern, war horse lawyer. He suggested that they hire Dover, and he would work alongside of him, gathering witnesses and working on the case. Bud said to bring him over to meet with them. Sam called Dover, and he came to Stilwell the next morning. They liked him enough to hire him. Mr. Dover had assigned Sam to Charles. The first time they met was when he went to bond Charles out of jail. Mr. Dover wanted Sam to keep a close eye on Charles and basically to be at his side at all times.

"Hey, Sam, my aunt tells me you and your associate are taking on my case. I've had some champion lawyers in the past. They successfully got me out of four charges of bank robbery. Do you think you can work some magic and get me out of this?" asked Charles.

"I sure am going to try. My associate, Mr. Dover has won many criminal cases, and I'm confident he will do his best for you, but first, we need to find out what they have on you. How did they know it was you, so quickly? You need to tell me everything that happened and then Dover and I will know what we're up against and how to get you out of it."

Charles told him about all about the bank robbery and how he had committed it. Sam reported everything to Dover. Sam told Dover that he liked Charles, but that he was taking pills and he didn't like that, saying that Charles would take enough pills to put a normal person into orbit for three or four days. Dover told Sam to stick to Charles like glue and to keep him out of trouble while he was out on bond. This worried Sam, since Charles had told him how he had robbed banks while out on bond to pay his lawyers in the past.

Every place Charles and Sam went, the FBI followed them. They put bugs on his cars, and Charles would just sell the car and get a new one. The feds were after him and this made Sam nervous. He didn't like the FBI following him all the time. He told Dover about it, and Dover told him not to worry, and that they weren't going to do anything to him.

Sam and Charles were having lunch in Moffet, at the café they liked. The FBI agents were sitting a few booths away from them trying to listen in on their conversation. Charles waved at them and asked them if they were picking up the bill.

"I like going to lunch with you because the FBI won't try to kill me if someone is with me, especially my attorney," said Charles.

"Are you serious? You think they would try to kill you?" Miles asked, turning and looking at the agents. He knew they could hear what Charles was saying.

"They have been trying to pin things on me for nine years now. They hate me. I think they've decided that if they can't catch me, they'll kill me. I've written a letter to J Edgar Hoover about it, and I want you to read it before I mail it today." Charles handed Sam the letter.

To whom it may concern,

I am Charles Parrott, age thirty-four, and I live in Stilwell, Oklahoma. I have been taped and bugged by your agents for the last week. I know that Bobby Lee Holmes helped the FBI and other law enforcement officers to do this. I know that hearsay and tape recordings are not legal evidence, so I have gone along with this little joke. I hope they go nuts trying to figure it out. I have been pushed around for the last eight years, and I am tired of it.

If I should die, they will have killed an unarmed
man, and that is why I am writing this letter. I am
also sending copies to the Adair County Sheriff's
Office and my lawyer, Sam Miles.

Yours truly,
Charles H. Parrott

"I don't know, Charles. Are you sure you want to mail this?"

"If they kill me, I need for others to know that I fear being
killed by the agents that can't catch me," Charles said.

"Okay, mail the letter."

"You have to keep them off my butt."

Dover told him that he had nothing to worry about, and as
far as keeping them off his butt, well he couldn't do anything
about that. Dover told him to quit being paranoid. They
weren't going to kill him when they had charges on him. Now
if he got him off the charge, then he could worry about that.

During the preliminary trial. The prosecutor, Calvin Rice,
built a solid case against Charles. He had witnesses who
placed him near the bank the night before the robbery. Two
girls aged fifteen and sixteen, who were with a bus full of basketball players and cheerleaders at a Dairy Queen, identified
him as a man they saw that night. When the FBI showed them
pictures of Charles Parrott, they only show them pictures of
Charles, no one else. The girls didn't positively identify him
at first, but the FBI continued to try to convince them, and it
worked. There was also a night watchman in the town, who
also identified Charles as a driver of a blue truck that he
followed around town.

The defense called their first witnesses, Liza Carol, who had
been good friends with Charles for years. She said that Charles

had been in her store three times the day of the robbery. She told the court he was there buying horse medicine, and then he came back later in the afternoon to buy candy for a late Valentine's Day gift for his mother and aunt.

They also call Patsy and her friend, Linda, to testify that they were with him the night before the robbery and the next day in the morning.

But the prosecution had these three witnesses that say they saw him close to Hartford that night and that was enough evidence that a court date was established.

Charles and Sam stayed in a motel in Fort Smith. They shared a room, and that morning before court Charles put a .38 pistol in his boot. Sam asked him why he needed to take the gun. His response was simply that he might need it. The room was full of police, state troopers, and FBI agents. It made Sam nervous.

When Sam told Dover about the gun in Charlie's boot, that morning, he said not to worry about it and that he probably wouldn't shoot anybody. Sam didn't stop worrying about that gun. Dover never seemed to worry much about anything.

Charles had a little mean streak in him if he got confronted. For some people, it took a minute when someone was pushing their buttons and for some people it didn't. When pressing Charles's buttons, it took a while, but when you finally pressed it too hard, you were in harm's way. Sam had seen Charles's temper flare with Agent Folger, and he certainly didn't want to get in the middle of him and the agent.

The trial was set, and they were going to hold court in the cafeteria of the high school in Greenwood, since the courthouse was destroyed by a recent tornado that had taken out half the town. Judge Jack James instructed the jury on July 8, 1968, and the trial began.

Calvin Rice, the prosecuting attorney, called his first witness, the vice president of the bank, Mr. Hazelton, and he tells what happened that morning when the bank got robbed.

The transcript:

Q Could you tell the jury what
happened on February 15, 1968?

A At ten minutes after ten that morning, we
were busy at the bank. There are two girls,
Miss Miller and Miss Bench that are working
with me. I was back behind the teller's cage
helping the girls when two armed men entered
the bank. One had a sawed-off shotgun, and
the other had a blue automatic pistol, and they
came behind the teller cages where we were
working. The one with the shotgun said this is
a holdup, and he pulled a sack from his pocket
and pitched it to Miss Bench, telling her to go
to the vault and to put the money in the sack.

The other man instructed Miss Miller and me to sit on the floor against a desk as he pulled the cash drawers and took the money and stuffed it into his jacket pockets, constantly keeping the pistol turned toward us and only taking his eyes off us for short moments. He was also keeping his eye on the front door.

When the man came out of the vault with Miss Bench, he told her to join us on the floor. Then he said for us to sit there for five minutes, and he said thank you very much and they left. Once the men were outside of the bank, I ran to the

window and saw the man with the shotgun raise the ski mask
just above his ears.

Q   Can you identify the man with
                 the shotgun in this courtroom?

A   Yes, sir. He is sitting right over
                 there to the extreme right.

Q   Let the record show that he has iden-
            tified Mr. Charles Parrott.

Q   What was the amount taken?

A   Forty-nine hundred and seventy dollars.

No further questions were asked, and it was Dover's turn.

Q Please describe the men who entered the
bank with as much detail as you can remember.
How they were dressed and if there were
any distinguishing things about them.

A The taller one was probably five-ten or more.
Fit looking and the other one was smaller, he
kept crouching down and it's hard to describe his
height or weight. The taller one drug his leg.

Q How were they dressed?

A Identical light blue coveralls and both had on
ski masks with only holes for the eyes and mouth.

Q You say you saw his face, but how could that
be if he only pulled the mask up to his ears. You
couldn't see the eyes or nose. Seems that would
be impossible. Can you say with a moral degree of
certainty and know that this is the man you saw?

Q Yes, sir, in my opinion it is.

The next witness for the prosecution was Nita Bench, and she
also told the same story about the entry, and she then went into
detail about the man with the shotgun throwing her the pillowcase. The prosecutor asked her to describe the pillowcase.
She told him it was dirty and dingy, and it had rust circles on it.
At this time the prosecutor asked to bring into evidence a dirty,
pillowcase with rust circles on it. It was admitted. And the
young teller identified it as the pillowcase from the robbery.

Up next was Janie Miller, also an employee of the bank. She
told of when the robbers left the bank. She said the taller one
said thank you as he went out the door. And after he exited,
he pulled his mask up as he was getting in the car. She called
out the license number to her coworker and the vice president,
who was already on the phone contacting the authorities. She
also noted the make of the car, a white Mercury Monterey. And
then she was asked if the man that robbed the bank was in the
courtroom, and she said yes and identified Charles Parrott.

The people working in the bank that day identified him as
one of the bank robbers. Then came the damning testimony of
a group of men who connected him with the getaway car. The
car had been stolen in Fayetteville.

Here is the testimony of Jimmy Davis when the prosecutor
questioned him:

Q Have you ever seen the man
seated at the defendants' table?

A Yes, sir, I have.

A My son and I noticed a car on our land. It
was a white Mercury Monterey. Someone had
parked it beside a stand of trees that runs along
the fence line. We walked up to the car and took
down the license plate number and saw that there
was a white lady's glove on the dashboard.

Q On that day, that you saw Charles Parrott in
your pasture, what did he say his name was?

A He said he was Joe Longshore, but I already
knew who he was. He was Charles Parrott. I don't
think he recognized me, but I had seen him at
rodeos and horse shows. I knew who he was.

Q And you wrote down the license number?

A Yes, sir.

The prosecution wished to have this entered as evidence.
    The court and the defense argued over the sheet of paper,
but it was admitted as evidence.
    They had a good case of connecting him to the getaway car
and that alias, Joe Longshore. It didn't look good for Charles.
    The prosecutor, Rice, called a witness that stated a blue
truck was seen leaving the area of the burned getaway car at
a high rate of speed. He was connecting all the dots. Rice also

called another witness that said he saw the white Mercury parked off the road the day before the robbery. The witness said he was up there dumping trash on the north side of the mountain when he noticed a light blue older Chevy truck pull up to the car and then drive away.

Next, Rice called the state trooper who arrested Charles on that day of February 15, 1968 for no tag on the Javelin and took him to the jail in Stilwell. He didn't mention that the FBI had asked to do this. There was no reason to take him to jail on traffic tickets, but the trooper said he couldn't confirm if the car was stolen and so he took him.

Rice called his next witness, the jailer at the Stilwell jail. The jailer went through his wallet and found a receipt with the name Joe Longshore. Again, connecting Charles to that alias that he used with the men when they saw him on their property with the getaway car. Charles screwed up using that car, and once the men confronted him about being on their property, he should have gotten rid of it. Maybe he was getting sloppy and not being as mentally prepared as he had been in the past.

The state rested their case. Now it was Dover's turn to bring witnesses. First up was Mrs. Liza Carol. He asked her if she saw Charles Parrott on the day of the bank robbery. She told the jury that she saw him the morning of the robbery, and then he came back twice in the afternoon, buying horse medicine on the first visit and then buying candy and back again to pick it up after it was gift wrapped. She stated that it was a late Valentine's Day gift for his mother.

Dover asked her if she was a close friend of Charles Parrott. And told him that he's an acquaintance of hers and that they don't ever visit socially.

Then Dover called Bud and Odessia's neighbor, Mrs. Dudley. She told the jury that she saw Charles the morning of the bank robbery on the road to his parents' home. She told Dover that she saw Charles driving the Javelin on the road.

The next witness for the defense was Mrs. Dana Atwater. She was employed at the department of welfare where Bud worked. Dover asked her if she was a friend of Charles, and she also told him that she was just a casual acquaintance. She tells the court she saw him twice that day. Once in the morning and once in the afternoon.

They told her that she could step down, and Dover called his next witness for the defense, Avery Ann Henson. Dover asked her a series of questions concerning her speaking with Parrott the day of the robbery. She told the jury that she had seen him that morning in front of her office and that they discussed him helping her husband with some cattle later in the week. Then she said she saw him again that afternoon on Main Street in Stilwell, where they spoke again.

Next up for the defense was Charles's mother, Odessia. She testified that her son came by her home that morning of the bank robbery asking if she had the title to his car, saying that the car company had mailed the title to her address. She told him that she had not received it. She also confirmed that he was going to get medicine for the horses that morning and that it was last time she saw him that day. When it was Rice's turn to question her, he only asked her three questions: did you only see him once that day, why did he come over, and what was he driving.

Dover called a mechanic as his next witness. The mechanic stated that the truck they had impounded was in such bad shape that there was no way Charles could have driven it all the ninety miles to Hartford and back. He stated that the truck basically had no brakes at all, when he'd examined it at the impound lot.

After the testimony of the mechanic, Dover rested his case. The judge called Dover and Charles to the bench and spoke to them about Charles not testifying. He told him it was his privilege not to testify and confirmed that he had the right to testify if he chose to. The judge asked him if he understood his rights, and Charles nodded his head.

Now it was Rice's turn, and he asked to bring evidence of the court transcript from the extradition hearing to rebut the alibi witnesses. The judge denied that this testimony by the defendant could be used against him, and Rice moved on.

Judge James asked Rice if he had any rebuttal witnesses, and Rice replied that he had two, possibly three. Rice called on Molly Steele, an employee of fifteen years of the store. She stated that she didn't see Parrott that morning in the store. When Dover questioned her and asked if she could see all the people that come and go in the store, she said that she could not, but she didn't see him that morning.

Next, Rice called Laura Thomas, another employee of the store. She also said that she didn't see Parrott that morning in the store. When Dover questioned her, he did a good job of establishing that when she was busy with her duties, and it was possible that she could have not noticed him in the store.

The FBI had interviewed every employee in the store and did their best to find at least one person that would testify that they didn't see him. The women didn't like testifying to discredit their boss, but they did.

The prosecution rested its case, and then the judge instructed the jury with a long, drawn-out speech and then Rice began his closing statements, summing up all of the damaging testimony and the solid connection to the getaway car and the alias, Longshore, being used. He laid it all out for the jury and handed it over to Dover.

Dover went into the alibis and how Parrott could not be in two places at one time. Stating that these witnesses knew him well and that the defense witnesses were mistaking him for someone else.

The jury were sent to deliberate his fate at 3:25 p.m. and returned at 4:30 p.m. with their verdict.

Judge James asked the foreman if they had arrived at a verdict and the foreman replied that they had and that it was unanimous. The judge warned the courtroom audience to remain quiet until the court adjourned, and the foreman handed the judge the paper with the verdict.

The judge asked Charles to stand as he read the verdict. "We, the jury, find the defendant guilty and sentence him to twelve years."

Judge James then instructed both attorneys, and Charles that there was a statute requiring two days before passing sentence upon a person convicted by a jury. This gave Charles two days to prepare to be sent to prison. The judge also offered them the choice of having the sentencing court date moved to Fort Smith, instead of the Greenwood High School cafeteria. They agreed to moving to the Fort Smith courtroom and set a time and day. The judge reminded Charles that his bond was still in effect and that he must be in the courtroom at two o'clock on that next Friday.

Charles had two days to say his goodbyes to his family and friends and get his things in order.

July 12, 1968, Fort Smith, Arkansas

THE COURT: Mr. Parrott, as you know you were charged with the offense of robbery. You entered a plea of not guilty, and you were tried by a jury in

the Greenwood district on Monday and Tuesday
of this week, and on this past Tuesday the jury
returned a verdict of guilty and fixed your sentence
at twelve years. Do you understand nature of
this charge and the proceedings had against you,
and the purpose of your being here today? Which
is to have this court pass sentence upon you?

MR. PARROTT: Yes, sir.

THE COURT: Do you have anything to say
before the sentence is pronounced?

MR PARROTT: No, sir, except that
people do make mistakes.

Dover had filed a motion for a new trial, as well as an appeal to
the Arkansas Supreme Court. Dover alleged that two witnesses
were observed talking to a juror during a lunch break. They
agreed to a court date to motion for the new trial to be set for
September to question the witnesses and the jurors that were
involved in the alleged misconduct.

The judge moved on to the sentencing and stated that
Charles Parrott would serve a period of twelve years in the
Arkansas State Penitentiary and that he was to surrender to a
sheriff for that purpose.

Dover piped in and asked for the defendant to be allowed
to continue under bond until the September court date. The
judge responded that his bond was up, and he didn't understand that he was entitled to a bond.

Dover educated the judge with law stating that he did
have the right to bond and that they had so many days from

this date to perfect their appeal. The judge remarked that he guessed he had been mistaken and that the court would give him whatever leave he is entitled to have, but instead of a September court date he would set the date for July 29th. They took a brief recess so that Dover could determine for sure that he could make that court date.

When they returned to the court room the prosecutor, Rice, stated that he wanted the names of the jurors who supposedly spoke with the witness. He then noticed that Parrott was not in the room. He asked Dover, "Where is Mr. Parrott?" Apparently, Charles was confident that Mr. Dover could keep him out of prison during the days before the motion for new trial and his appeal. Or maybe he was outside the courthouse ditching the gun that he had in his boot.

Charles had two more weeks of freedom.

OUT ON BOND

Reba Sue was furious with Charles. He'd told her that he was running the grocery store and that he was living a straight life. He told her he was done playing the game with the FBI. Down deep, she didn't believe him. After she heard about the trial, she knew he was being reckless. She wondered how Patsy was handling this. She knew how it felt to love him and fear losing him for his crimes. They may lose him for twelve years. Toni, Susan, and Charles Lee wouldn't have a father. She'd have no child support to care for them.

She decided that she would accept Roy Keen's proposal. She had known Roy for a long time, and she needed someone solid in her life. He had traveled from Stilwell to see her every other weekend and he continued to include her children on many of their dates. He was good to the kids and that was the deciding factor for her. Roy was offered a good job in Oklahoma City with the state. He said he could get her on at the welfare department if they were to marry and move there. She'd lived with her parents for the past year and half, and she felt that it was time to move on with her life. Roy could provide stability for her and the children.

She had heard that Charles was out on bond, while his attorneys were working to get him a new trial. She didn't tell the children anything and wouldn't until she knew if he was going to prison or not. It was going to be hard to explain to them about their father and what was going on.

Just two weeks after Charles had been granted an extension on his bond and waiting for the Arkansas Supreme Court to hear his appeal, Charles went and robbed the Farmers Bank in Hackett, Arkansas on February 27, 1968. The bank was only fifteen miles from the Hartford bank that he had robbed and been convicted for. He was on a mission to mess with the FBI.

Charles stole another white Mercury, just like the one he used in Hartford and started planning the Hackett robbery. He covered the car with hay in Mitch Murray's barn in Stilwell to hide it until the day came to rob the bank

This time Tommy was going to be his partner. Charles coached him, telling him to speak with a Mexican accent and telling him to ask where the phone was by using sign language and then to rip it out of the wall. Other than asking for the phone, he was to be quiet and watch the door and the people inside.

Charles saw on the news that snow was in the forecast and that triggered him to go rob the bank. It slowed down the lawmen, but not him. Cotton came by, and Charles asked him to go along and drive them out of Hackett. Of course, Cotton was game. He would never turn down a job with Charles.

Charles met Cotton that morning at Mitch's garage. Rosey was involved also as his decoy, and he had arrived earlier that morning to meet them there. Cotton pulled his truck into the bay and Mitch closed the garage door. Then Charles showed up and parked out front. Mitch went out to greet Charles and he handed Mitch a box and they went inside. Once inside Mitch gave the box back to Charles. It held the guns, money sacks and disguises. Charles gave Rosey his hat, sunglasses, and white shirt. Rosey would hang around the garage pretending to be Charles, sitting with his back facing the large window. The FBI sat there watching him, as Charles laid down in the seat of Cotton's truck and they pulled away.

Tommy was a bundle of nerves driving over there with Charles driving and Cotton following in his truck.

"Tommy, you gonna be okay? Would you rather I take Cotton in the bank with me?"

"No, I'm fine. I can do it. I want to do it," Tommy answered as he lit up one cigarette after the other.

"Okay. We will be in and out in no time. Just do as I told you, and things will go smoothly."

Charles was excited to pull this one off. He would make a fool out of that agent sitting back at Mitch's garage. He had told Rosey to leave the garage in his truck in an hour and half and drive out to the store and see Patsy. He was to go in the back door, so the agent wouldn't get a good look at him. Patsy would lock the front door, and if the agent came up to the door, Rosey would slip out the back, while she opened the door. The agent would have no access to a phone, and he wouldn't know about the robbery until the guys were back in Stilwell. Charles told Rosey he would call the store when it was time to head back to Mitch's garage and they would trade clothes. It was a perfect plan. The FBI agent would be his alibi.

They arrived in Hackett and went to a cemetery on the outskirts of the small town.

"Tommy, you ready for your first bank robbery?" asked Cotton.

"I guess you're never ready, unless you're Charlie Parrott," said Tommy.

"If you're scared, I'll do it," said Cotton with a grin.

"Shut the hell up," Tommy responded.

Charles got out two dark overcoats, two fedora hats, bandanas, dark gloves for both, and two cloth sacks for the money. When he pulled out the sawed-off shotgun and the pistol, Tommy's eyes got big. Charles grinned. He loved Tommy and got a kick out of him coming along. He knew he was afraid. They all were the first time they came along.

"Okay, let's go get that money. I got lawyers to pay," said Charles.

There was only one lady employee inside the bank. This gave Tommy a little comfort. Charles went into his bank robbing talking, and after he was finished having her empty the tills and the vault, Tommy chimes with his attempt at a Mexican accent, while motioning like he is dialing and putting a phone to his ear.

"Ringy, ringy, ringy," Tommy says, and the lady shows him the phone. He jerks the phone cord out of the wall, and she gasps.

"Ma'am, I'm going to place you in the vault. I won't lock it if you promise me, you won't come out for ten minutes," said Charles.

"Yes, sir, I promise I won't."

He walked her back to vault, told her thank you and closed the heavy door.

Tommy had just exited the bank with Charles right behind him when Charles slipped on the icy sidewalk and fired off the shotgun. They hurried to the car, knowing that someone in the small town had heard the blast.

"So much for having a head start," muttered Charles.

Tommy looked out the rear window and didn't see anyone coming as Charles was traveling pretty damn fast for the road condition.

"Slow down. No one's coming. If you wreck, we're screwed," said Tommy.

"Take off the overcoat, gloves, hats and put the guns in the sack with the money," said Charles as he wrestled to get out of his coat.

Charles slowed down and pulled over after a few miles down the dirt road to the cemetery. He hopped out and dropped the bags into the pre-dug hole and covered it with a big rock.

When they got to the pickup spot, Cotton had the truck running and ready to go. They hopped in and put on their cowboy hats and off they went down the road, just a bunch of old cowboys in a truck.

"Damn, Tommy, you were pretty damn cool in there. I think you were the coolest of all my first-time partners," Charles said.

"It was going fine, until your damn gun went off outside. Thank God, you didn't shoot me," declared Tommy.

"Oh crap," Cotton said.

"Sorry about that," said Charles as he concentrated on his driving.

Charles pulled onto the highway and there wasn't a vehicle on the road, then he hit the back roads, just to make sure they didn't find any roadblocks.

"I sure as hell hope that there isn't a roadblock before we cross the Arkansas River. If those lawmen were smart, they be there waiting for us," Charles said.

As they came over the hill approaching the river the men were sitting on the edge of their seat, i anticipating a roadblock. They all let out a long sigh of relief when there weren't any cops in sight. Once they were on the bridge, it was solid ice. Charles guided the truck as best he could, and at one point, they were sliding sideway for about twenty yards, but Charles corrected the truck and they made it to the other side. He pulled over at a gas station and called Patsy at the store. The code was to let the phone ring twice and hang up. They knew their phones were tapped, and this was the code to send Rosey on his way back to Murray's garage.

"Rosey, they're on their way! They made it," Patsy exclaimed.

"Of course, they made it," Rosey said as he walked toward the back door with a grin on his face.

When they got back to Stilwell, Cotton took over driving, and Charles laid down in the seat hiding from the agent that was sitting across the street. He pulled up to the station and Mitch raised the garage door so they could pull inside. Charles and Rosey changed clothes and they all had a good laugh at the agent who was sitting across the street.

Murray slapped Tommy on the back and said, "So, how was it?"

"I don't think it was a very big take, but I got my one and done," said Tommy.

"Damn, Tommy, you did great, but I know it's not for everybody. I'm just glad we got to do one together. Make sure you pick up the newspaper tomorrow to see what we got in that sack," said Charles.

The next day they read that the take was one thousand three hundred dollars. Not a lot, but for Charles it was more about making fools of the FBI. To him, it was worth a million dollars.

When Agent Folger finally heard from his agent that was tracking Parrott, he was disappointed to hear that he had watched Parrott all day and there was no way he could have robbed the Hackett bank. Folger had noticed that the getaway car was exactly the same model as Parrott had used in Hartford, and he wondered if Charles had sent him a message by doing that. Maybe he fooled the agent that was trailing him, but he didn't fool him. He'd bet money that Parrott robbed the bank in Hackett.

Two months after the robbery with Tommy, Charles was ready to rob another bank. He had to rob as many as he could before he went to prison in Arkansas. He knew he was running out of time. His appeal on the conviction on the Hartford bank will most likely be denied. He was living free on borrowed time. He could run and go to Mexico, but then he would never see his kids, and he would be a fugitive for the rest of his life. That wasn't something he could do.

His children were in Oklahoma City now with Reba Sue. She had agreed to let him have the kids over the Thanksgiving vacation, and she drove down to Golden to her parents' home. Charles came over to pick up the kids.

"Charles, you don't look good," she said.

"I haven't been sleeping well. I have that prison time hanging over me, and I feel like I'm going insane right now."

"You know that I care about you and that the kids need you. If you go to prison, I'll bring them to see you. I'll always stand up for you and be loyal to you, no matter what happens."

"I care about you and the kids too. I'm sorry that I messed everything up for us. I don't blame you for divorcing me. I was an awful husband and sometimes not the best father."

"The husband part yes, but the father part no. They love you to no end. They were so happy to hear that they would be spending the long weekend with you. What are your plans?"

"I'm going to take them out to the movies tonight and I want to take them hunting with me and some friends. We'll be camping out Thursday night and I think they'll have fun. Today, we are going to shoot targets and see how well they do. I'd like to spend time with Toni Lynne. She's three years old now and doesn't even know me. Could I pick her up on Saturday?"

"Charles, I know what goes on at deer camp, and I'm not sure that's a good idea. Y'all will be drinking and who knows what else. As for having Toni Lynne on Saturday, that will be fine."

"Don't worry, Patsy and Jonesy's wife, Peggy, will be there to watch over the kids. I promise you it will be okay. If you like, I can have Patsy call you to go over the hunting trip."

"Have her call me, and we'll talk about it."

Charles gathered up the kids' suitcases, and they headed over to the motel that he and Patsy were staying at. Patsy's kids were with their father, and Susan was disappointed that her stepsister, Robyn wasn't there. They assured her that she would see them on Saturday and that tonight they were going to a movie in Broken Bow. They let Susan pick the movie and she wanted to see *Chitty Chitty Bang Bang*. They had a nice dinner before the show and afterward, they got ice cream at the Dairy Queen. While eating ice cream, Susan told him how much she hated Oklahoma City and that this was the best time she'd had since they'd moved. She told him that the kids at school made fun of her because she dressed like a cowgirl. Charles's eyes welled up.

He imagined how tough it was for them. Being country kids and moving to the big city was traumatic. He could tell by the stories they told him that they were unhappy and that was hard to take in.

Patsy called Reba Sue the next day to talk to her about the hunting trip. Reba Sue told her that Charles Lee could go hunting with them, but she would prefer that Susan be dropped back at her grandparents' house.

When they target practiced, Charles Lee proved to be a good shot. Charles had bought him a nice rifle as an early Christmas present. He was thirteen now and he was excited that he'd finally get to go hunting with his dad and show him that he could bag a deer.

The deer camp was all set up just north of Broken Bow near the mouth of Bar Creek, that flows into the Mount Fork River. The women had a pot of coffee going on the hot coals of the campfire, and they had cooked up bacon and eggs on a big iron skillet. They had slept in the camper and some tents the night before and woke at the break of dawn. The men were ready to get to their deer stands. Charles had brought his motorcycle along to take them out to their individual spots deep in the woods. He took Charles Lee first out to an area where there was a nice open clearing just beyond the tree where his stand was.

"I'm giving you the best spot. Don't move from this spot until I get back. I'm going to take Jonesy to his spot and later on I'm going to take the motorcycle to the other side of the clearing over there and run those bucks your way."

"All right, Dad, and thanks for the spot. Hope you get one too. I'll see you later," he said.

Charles told him good luck, reminding him to stay put until he returned. He didn't want him wandering in the woods with all the hunters in the area. He roared off on the motorcycle and headed back to camp.

When Charles returned to the campsite, he gave his motorcycle helmet and jacket to Jonesy.

"Jonesy, in around an hour I want you to ride the motorcycle around to the other deer camps and wave at anyone you see. Then I want you to ride over to the other side of the clearing from Charles Lee's deer stand and ride around reeving the engine, so that Charles Lee hears you over there. After that head back to deer camp and wait for me and Patsy to come back," said Charles.

"You sure you want to do this? What if you don't come back? What am I supposed to tell Charles Lee if that happens?" asked Jonesy.

"Tell him I wrecked the motorcycle, and you took me to the hospital, then take him back to Reba Sue," said Charles.

Charles and Patsy got into the truck and went to pick up the car that Jonesy had stolen. Patsy followed him in the truck to an abandoned old house outside of Hartshorne, Oklahoma.

They arrived at the getaway spot, and he put on the trench coat and stocking cap with the holes for the mouth and eyes cut out. He had told Patsy that if he didn't return in twenty minutes, she was to leave.

When he entered the bank there were several people inside. One man was standing at the teller's booth, and Charles pushed him aside. The man turned, thinking this was a joke and kicked Charles in the leg. Charles hit him hard upside of the head with the stock of the sawed-off shotgun. Then he told him to go sit in a corner or he would blow his brains out. Everyone inside the bank was frightened.

"I want all the money in this bank, and I want it fast," he yelled at the teller and the bank president.

"Get to work and fill these sacks!"

He threw the sacks on the floor, and they picked them up and started emptying the teller cages then handed them to Charles. He told them to go to the vault and empty it also. The sacks were heavy. Charles knew this was a good take.

Patsy died a thousand deaths waiting for Charles. Just as she questioned whether she could leave there without him, he came roaring up the road toward her. She jumped in the truck and started it. He'd already dropped the money, gun, and disguise in the hidey hole.

"Honey, that was a good one. My sacks have never been so full," he said.

"Which way should I go?" she asked as he came to the highway.

"Turn left."

"Back toward Hartshorne?"

"Yeah, there's no way they have a roadblock up yet, and it's the quickest way to get back to Broken Bow."

As they pulled into town, people and cars were flying around the town square. It was crazy, and she was scared to death. Once they were five miles out of town, they saw the cops speeding toward Hartshorne. They flew right past them with lights and sirens. Charles smiled at her and assured her they would be okay and to keep driving at a good pace. She got them back to the camp within an hour. Charles was in a great mood and very calm. He laughed with Jonesy and his wife telling them he couldn't wait to read the newspaper tomorrow and find out what the amount of money was. He hopped on his motorcycle to fetch Charles Lee.

When he pulled up his son climbed down from his stand with a sour look on his face.

"Did you see that big buck I ran this way?" Charles asked. "He was the biggest buck I've ever seen,"

"No, Dad, I didn't see him. I took several shots at young bucks but missed. It just wasn't my day I guess."

Charles Lee had such a deflated look. His dad put his arm around him and told him that no one bagged a deer today and that he wasn't alone. This seemed to make Charles Lee feel a little better.

When they returned to camp, they packed everything up and headed back to Broken Bow. As they were coming upon where the road crossed a creek, they saw several men standing on the creek bank. Their truck had stalled in the high water. The men were drunk as skunks. Charles saw another opportunity for an additional alibi. He offered to pull them out with a chain attached to the bumper of his truck and he looked at his watch, saying he had to hurry. He said that it was two o'clock, when it was really three thirty in the afternoon and convinced them of the time by saying they had to hurry because he had to be in town by two thirty to get his son back to his mom.

The next morning Jonesy came over with the local paper, and the article said the amount was forty-two thousand dollars. This was the biggest take Charles had ever had and now he sat and waited for the FBI to show up. He and Patsy were ready for them.

Agent French and a new guy that Charles didn't know came to the motel where they were staying. French asked a lot of questions while the young agent wrote things down.

"Who were you deer hunting with?" French asked.

"My son and Jonesy Monson, an old friend of mine. And my wife and Jonesy's wife, Peggy were there also. I didn't rob the Hartshorne Bank. I don't even know where that is. How far is it from here?"

"One hundred miles," said French. "And I have no doubt that with your driving skills that you could have done it. The thing that I would have a hard time believing is that you would endanger your own son, and if you did, you're a real son of bitch."

Charles felt a pang of hurt and anger and looked at French like he wanted to kill him. French returned the look. These two hated each other, and French's patience was worn slick. French turned to leave, and the young agent followed him.

"Did you get all those names?" French asked the young agent.

"Yes, sir. I have them all written down."

"I want you to get the bait money serial numbers from Hartshorne and find out where the Monson's bank at and where they shop at. Give them a copy of the serial numbers and tell them to call you if they use any of those bills. The same with Parrott. One of them is going to spend that money, and then we'll have them."

Less than two weeks later, Jonesy's wife Peggy, paid off a car loan with three of the marked bills. Charles had told Jonesy and Peggy not to spend any of the money for at least three months, but Peggy had disobeyed.

FBI went to the bank where Peggy paid the loan. They had the evidence they needed to arrest Jonesy and Peggy. Agent Folger and French were pleased. They didn't have Charles Parrott, but they had his accomplice.

Jonesy and Peggy were picked up and arrested for bank robbery. When Charles found out about the arrest, he knew that they would be coming for him and Patsy. Patsy was terrified of going to prison.

Charles knew that Reba Sue was going to kill him for involving their son. He was ashamed of what he'd done. His recklessness was going to destroy everyone he loved.

When the FBI showed up at Charles Lee's school and the principal allowed them to question him, Reba Sue was livid, threating to sue the school and the FBI. She couldn't believe that Charles has involved their son.

When Charles got the news about Jonesy and Peggy being arrested, his blood boiled. And now he knew that there was marked money, and he would have to have all of the money laundered. He knew a bail bondsman by the name of Saul Chadwick that could take care of that for him.

He immediately took the money to him. He would have to be careful about that because the FBI were keeping a constant tail on him now. He had the money buried back behind his Aunt Polly's house and he'd get it to Saul as soon as he could.

Just as Charles was about to close the grocery store that evening, Reba Sue came charging in the door and slapped the fire out of him.

"How could you do this to our son?" she screamed.

"Reba Sue, I didn't rob that bank. Jonesy—"

"Shut up, you liar. You know and I know what you did. You used your own son as your alibi. I hate you. Charles Lee came home from school today, and he told me that he'd been pulled out of class and questioned by an FBI agent. You will never see your kids again. If I had a gun, I'd shoot you right now. I hope you burn in hell"

She turned to leave, and Charles tried to stop her. She spit in his face and shoved him out of the way. Tears were running down her face as she got in her car and peeled out of the parking lot.

After she left, Charles wept and knew she was right. He was out of control.

The next day, Charles stole a big truck that delivered groceries to the local grocers. He knew the truck route because the driver brought his groceries for the store, and Charles had asked him how long his route was when he first started running the store. He drove the truck up Maxwell Mountain Road, just up from his store. He stopped in to see his friend, Bobby Redcorn, and told him he needed help emptying the truck.

"Charlie, why are you emptying this truck here in the middle of nowhere?" asked Bobby.

"I want you to let the people know up here that I want them to have all this food."

"But you run a grocery store?"

"Yeah, and I know that a lot of people up here run out of their food stamps, and I want to help them. Just tell them to not tell anyone since I stole the truck. I just need to do a good deed. I got some penitence to pay."

They got the truck unloaded, and Charles drove out of there as the sun went down. The community of Greasy decided that they liked Charles Parrott.

One afternoon not long after the grocery delivery, a native man came into the store and told Charles that there was a man up on the mountain watching the store with binoculars. Charles saddled up his horse and rode up there. He startled a young FBI agent as he walked up on him.

"Who you looking for?" Charles asked.

"I'm just looking at the mountains," the young man answered.

"You hiked all this way off the road to look at the mountains? Kid, you can just tell me that you're watching me."

"All right. I was watching you."

"You tell French that you can just sit in my parking lot if you need to. You're going to get ate up by chiggers and tics out here. Maybe even get bit by a rattler."

"Thank you, sir," said the agent.

"What's your name?" asked Charles.

"Jarad Romey."

"Okay, Romey, I'll see you around.

The next morning, Romey was sitting out beside the store. He came in at noon and asked Patsy to make him a bologna sandwich and bought a Coke and some chips. He asked where Charles was, and she told him he was out back riding his horse. She was very cool to him and didn't want to make any small talk. When he pulled off the lot around five that evening, he heard breaking glass. He stopped the car and saw a shattered pop bottle that someone had put by his tire. He examined the tire and then drove off. He wondered who put it there. A few minutes later Patsy's son, Ricky came out and saw the broken glass and was disappointed that the agent hadn't gotten a flat.

The next day when Romey came back, it was a repeat of the day before. This time Ricky put two pop bottles under his wheel. Romey pulled out and again heard the glass breaking. He got out and examined the tire again, shaking his head. He didn't think a grown man would do this. Then he saw Ricky peering around the corner of the store and knew who was trying to cause him trouble. Romey would eventually stop coming to the store. It seemed there was nothing to find out there.

THE BURN BAR

As the days and weeks went by, Charles thought maybe he would get away with the Hartshorne robbery. Jonesy and Peggy weren't giving him up. He was thankful for that. He was laying low and waiting for his appeal court date on the Hartford case.

In March, Charles met some guys from Missouri that had some ideas about how to commit a bank burglary. They had convinced Charles that this would be easy and that they could help him acquire what they called a burn bar. It was an explosive device that could supposedly burn through the vault door, opening it without burning the money inside. He paid them five hundred dollars for the device, and he also bought a welding set that he would need to operate the burn bar.

Charles and Patsy went over to see Tommy and his wife, Anna. Charles came in with the burn bar. It was a long metal bar with wires attached to it.

"What the hell is that thing?" asked Tommy.

"It's a burn bar. I'm going to take this bar, and I'm going to burglarize a bank, and it will be the easiest bank job I'll ever do."

"But you don't know nothing about this thing. Can you try it out before you try it?" asked Anna.

"No, it can only be used one time from what the guys from Missouri told me."

"I think you better stick to what you do best. I don't think this is a good idea, Charles. You just don't know enough about this thing. You haven't seen it work," Tommy pleaded.

He left that burn bar behind Tommy's couch for a couple of weeks. Tommy repeatedly tried to talk him out of it, but Charles wouldn't listen. Charles recruited Tommy's niece's husband to go with him. A young man by the name of Cordell Mitchell. The plan was to burglarize a bank in Carney, Oklahoma. Tommy told Cordell that no matter what happens, stay with Charles and he'd be okay.

April 3, 1969

It was 2:15 in the morning when Charles and Cordell approached the bank in Carney, Oklahoma. Charles was on a motorcycle and Cordell was driving the truck with a camper on the back holding the burn bar and the welding equipment. They slowly drove by and then went up to a cemetery outside of Carney where Charles left the motorcycle and planned to ride it out of there after the burglary of the bank. They would split up and meet back in Stilwell.

The bank president, J.R. White, was awakened by the speaker next to his bed. The bank had microphones as a security system that were wired to the bank president's home. He heard a truck with a loud muffler and a motorcycle. He thought this was odd. There's a city ordinance that doesn't allow any motorcycle riding in town after ten o'clock, so as not to disturb the town residents. He heard them drive off and laid there pondering on whether he should call the sheriff and decided not to.

Ten minutes later, he heard a loud cracking and popping noise. He could also hear muffled voices. He called the sheriff and summoned his help. Then he got dressed and got his rifle and told his wife to keep listening to the speaker. He called the sheriff once more and told him to hurry and that he was scared to go down to the bank alone.

Charles and Cordell had pried the door open to the bank and got the hoses and welding tank out of the truck, dragging them inside. Charles placed the burn bar on the vault door and hooked up the wires and hose. Nothing happened, the device didn't work.

"Don't you think we better get out of here?" asked Cordell.

Charles was mad and threw his cowboy hat at the vault. He and Cordell took the equipment and got back in the truck. Charles revved the engine and rammed the door of the bank with the truck several times. He was furious.

Mr. White was sitting down the street from the bank. He didn't want to approach these criminals. The vice president of the bank also had speakers, and he had gotten in his car to come to the bank. He saw the truck with the camper going down the highway and he turned around to follow the truck, but it was going at a high rate of speed, and he knew he couldn't keep up with them. He turned around and went back into Carney, where he saw Mr. White and two police cars in front of the bank. He told the officers the direction that the truck was headed, and they took off to find it.

Charles saw the man chasing him out of town and knew that the police would be coming for him. He told Cordell to break the back glass between the truck and the camper to crawl into the back of the truck camper and to throw everything out the back as he drove down the road. Cordell threw a shotgun, the oxygen tank, the cart that was attached to the tank, a duffle bag and goggles. He crawled back through the window after he'd thrown everything out. Charles pulled over.

"Cordell you can just get out of this now. I'll see you in Stilwell. If I get caught, I don't want you with me."

Cordell thought about what Tommy had said. Stay with Charlie.

THE BURN BAR 265

"No, I'm riding this out with you," he said.

"Okay this could get nasty," Charles replied.

Charles saw lights coming up from behind at a high rate of speed. They were coming for him. He accelerated and was hitting eighty miles per hour on the dirt road. He would lose the cops after a one-hour chase. No one could outdrive him on dirt roads, and he was feeling good and thought they had it made. That's when he came up over a hill, and there was a roadblock on Highway 66. He could have tried to run through it or turn around, but the road was too narrow and there were deep ditches on each side. He pulled over and gave the cop his driver's license. He and Cordell were arrested and taken to the Oklahoma County jail in Oklahoma City.

Agent Folger had been called immediately after the arrest. He went to the scene where they found the articles thrown from the back of the truck and he asked the man that lived near the scene if there were any cemeteries nearby. He knew Charles Parrott's ways and he was sure that he would find a getaway vehicle there. He was right. There at the cemetery was a blue Honda motorcycle and a blue helmet.

The motorcycle was registered in the name of Charles Parrott and so was the Dodge truck with the camper. Folger found two walkie-talkies on the road and a duffle bag with a dynamite fuse and detonator cord in it. After his investigation, he went to the jail where they were holding the two men. Charles refused to talk to him and asked for an attorney. Folger had two guards hold him while he cut hair off his head. He wanted to compare the hair in the cowboy hat left at the scene. He made him remove his boots and compared them to shoes found on the side of the road by the welding equipment. They never found the burn bar.

"I've got you this time," muttered Folger.

Charles was bleary eyed from no sleep, and he was irritated with himself. He was a shell of the man he used to be. He wasn't the brilliant bank robber anymore. He had been caught and they were going to make this stick. He knew prison time was in his near future, and he would probably never see his children again. Reba Sue would be disgusted with him after this screw up.

Patsy was panicked. She went to Oklahoma City to see Charles in the county jail. He told her to go to see Reba Sue and ask her if she could give him an alibi, if she had any ideas on how he could get out of this. Patsy thought it was crazy to go to see his ex-wife, but she did it.

Reba Sue opened the door, and when she saw Patsy, she embraced her. She knew how it felt to be in her shoes. They went inside and came up with a plan and met with Charles's lawyer, Joe Dollins, a public defender. Patsy didn't have the money to hire a good attorney because Charles had given the bail bondsman in Sallisaw all the money from the Hartshorne robbery to launder and he had not returned a dime of it yet. And he probably never would now that this had happened. They cooked up a plan with the attorney.

Just two months before his trial began, on April 24th a grand jury indicted Charles and Patsy for the bank robbery in Hartshorne. They said they had found Charles's fingerprints on a newspaper that was left in the getaway car. They arrested Patsy and set her bond at five thousand dollars. She was terribly afraid that Jonesy and his wife had turned on them. Her family paid the bond, and she was released.

The day of the Carney bank trial the witnesses for the state give their testimony and it looked very damning.

The judge in the case was the same judge that was on the Valliant case back in 1961. Charles was worried about this. He knew that the judge would like nothing more than for him to be found guilty and sent to prison.

The prosecutor's case was solid, and next up was the defense. Mr. Dollins started with Cordell's wife.

She testified that Charlie and Cordell had gone to Oklahoma City to see Charles's children and that they were planning to go to Tulsa to see Charles's dad, Bud Parrott, on the way back home. Bud had been transferred to the Tulsa office and had been living in an apartment there. That would have put them on the road from Oklahoma City to Tulsa.

Then Tommy Porter's wife, Anna, was called to testify. She said that Charles and his wife, Patsy, and her children stayed with them the night of March 25, 1969. This testimony was to contradict the testimony of a man seeing him in Carney earlier in the week before the Carney break-in. She told the court that Charles said someone bad was after him and he didn't feel safe going home with Patsy and the kids and so she had invited them to stay at their home that night.

Dollins called Reba Sue to the stand.

Q Did you have occasion to see or talk to Mr. Parrott on the night of the April third?

A I didn't see him, but I talked with him on the phone around seven that night.

Q Was Mr. Parrott coming to your house that night?

A Yes, he wanted to visit the children.

Q Tell us what happened.

A I said all right, but he and I had been having
a little trouble and so, before he got there, I
took the children to the drive-in movie.

Q What time did you take them to the movie?

A Around nine o'clock.

Q What time did you arrive back at home?

A Around midnight.

Q Now do you know whether Mr.
Parrott had been there or not?

A I wouldn't have, except for he left me a note,
attached to the clothespin on my mailbox. The
mailbox is next to my front door. The note said he
was disappointed that we were gone and that he
had put my child support payment in the mailbox.

Q And was the payment there?

A Yes, sir.

Q You didn't see him then that night?

A No, I didn't.

Q Is it unusual for Mr. Parrott to come over
in the evening to visit with the children?

A No, he came to see them often. I mean,
he always wants to visit with them.

Q Did anyone see him come to your house?

A Yes, I was talking with my neighbor the next
day, and I asked her if she saw him come by. I
was curious if he was alone when he came by. I
wondered if his aunt was with him. She loved the
kids so much, and I felt bad if I had disappointed
her by taking the kids away when he was supposed
to come. My neighbor told me she did see him
and that he was with another man, not his aunt.

Now she was cross-examined by
the prosecuting attorney.

Q Now, Mrs. Parrott, did you tell this jury that
Charles Parrott was at your house at seven o'clock?

A No, no. He couldn't have been
there at seven o'clock.

Q On April third?

A No he called me from Stilwell at seven
o'clock asking to come see the children.

Q Wait so how did you know he
was calling you from Stilwell?

A Because when he called, there was an operator
on the line, and I asked the operator who
was calling, and she said, Stilwell and I asked
who the party was that was calling? He was
calling from a payphone most likely. I didn't
accept the call. We had been arguing lately.

Q You didn't take the phone call?

A No, but he called right back, and I took the
call and he told me he wanted to come see
the children that night. I told him okay, but
then since we had been arguing I had taken
the kids to the drive-in. We tend to bicker
back and forth like a divorced couple does.

Q Did you attend his preliminary hearing?

A Yes, I did. I came in about thirty
minutes before it was over.

Q And why did you attend the hearing?

A He is the father of my children, and
I wondered what had happened. We
have three children together.

Q Do you remember talking to
the FBI agent. Mr. Folger?

A Yes, I do.

Q Did you mention anything with him
about what you have testified to today?

A About this thing that happened at Carney?

Q Uh-huh.

A I don't think that anything was
mentioned about that because I don't
think I was asked anything about that.

Q You certainly had an opportunity to discuss
with him … didn't he mention that he was going
to talk to you about the Carney State burglary?

A No, he mentioned that he was going to talk to
me about something else. My former husband's
past. That's what he was interested in.

Q But you were aware of the fact…

The defense attorney interrupted, "May I approach the
bench, Your Honor. His interrogation is getting into some of
the conversation this agent had with her about some other
trouble the defendant might have been in. He's treading on
dangerous territory."

Reba Sue couldn't believe how stupid the attorney representing Charles was. He shouldn't have intervened.

The judge asked the prosecutor what he was driving at here
and warned him, by saying, "You're not proceeding properly.
If you want to point out that she made some statement to the
agent that is contrary to what she has testified here today,

then do it. But you're questioning her about her discussion with an FBI agent that could include her former husband's previous troubles, and she is pulling you right into a mistrial. She can ruin your case if you don't step back on this type of questioning."

"I don't want a mistrial, Your Honor," he responded, and they left the bar.

Q What is the name of this neighbor
of yours that saw Mr. Parrott?

A Mrs. Marie Dow.

Q And do you have her phone number
and contact information?

A Her husband was stationed at Tinker Air Force
Base, and they just moved a week ago to Guam.
I'm not sure how to contact her, but I'm sure you
could find out from his commanding officer.

Q Is your purpose of testifying for Charles
Parrott here an effort to help him?

A The purpose of my testimony is to tell the truth.
I don't have any other choice than to do that.

Q Did you discuss this case with
anybody else, Mrs. Parrott?

A Now when you asked me a
while ago if Mr. Folger—

Q No, I am asking you.

A Do you mean when I came to the preliminary and Mr. Folger and his agents came at me?

Q No. I want to ask you if you just discussed this case with Charles Parrott?

A I have not seen Charles until today. I haven't been near the jail, and I'm sure you can verify that.

Q That is all, Mrs. Parrott.

Then Dollins called Patsy to the stand.

She testified that they had stayed with Tommy Porter and his wife on the night that the man said that he saw Charles in Carney a few days before the break-in.

She also talked about how Charles had wrecked the truck the week before in Southeast Oklahoma while visiting her family and going to a dance where her brother's band was playing. And how her head had hit the back window of the truck, breaking the glass.

Dollins presented a statement written by the sheriff stating that the truck had been involved in an accident and a receipt for the money paid to the farmer, whose fence had been damaged.

When it was the prosecutor's turn to question her, he made some accusations about how Cordell Bench had been with her sister during the weekend of the dance and the accident. Patsy denied those statements.

He asked her if her husband took long trips, and she replied that he did not. Then he stated well how do you put five thousand miles on a brand-new truck in forty-five days.

He asked her if her husband owned a motorcycle, and she told him that he didn't at the time, but he had in the past.

The next person to testify was Cordell Bench. He was going to take the stand, which is risky.

Dollins started off with Bench's military service and how he had never been in any trouble. He went over the details of the trip to see Charles's children. He also told how Charles's mother, Odessia, asked him to go with Charles, telling him how Reba Sue and Charles quarreled over the children and that it might be better if Charles had someone with him.

Bench told of how, on the way to Tulsa, they were pulled over in Chandler and arrested. He told them they didn't go to Carney and they had been on Highway 66 for most of the way.

When he was cross-examined by Burleigh and questioned about his interview with FBI agent Folger, Burleigh asked him why he refused to tell Folger anything. Burleigh told him that he knew his rights and wasn't going to talk to anyone without an attorney present.

Burleigh brought out the exhibit of the paper that they said was in his wallet. The paper had the drawing of a burn bar, the supposed implement that they used to try to get into the vault. Bench denied that it was in his wallet.

After Bench's testimony, Agent Folger, testified about how he took the drawing of the burn bar out of Bench's wallet. And then they brought back a special agent with the FBI to confirm that the drawing in Bench's wallet was that of a burn bar used by thieves to burn though the thickest of safes and vaults.

After this rebuttable of witness testimony by the prosecutor, the defense attorney rested his case, without a closing argument. He wasn't a good attorney, and he didn't seem to have much faith in his client.

The jury left the courtroom with their instructions from the judge at 9:25 that morning and returned at 10:25, only taking an hour to reach their conclusion. The verdict for both men was guilty as charged. The jury did not have to decide on punishment. The judge would determine that, and he sentenced Cordell Bench to seven years and would give Charles the maximum sentence. The judge would get his retribution on Charles for escaping the charges on the court's mistake back in 1961. That payback was twenty years in Leavenworth.

After the sentencing on Carney, Charles's parents and Aunt Polly wept openly in the courtroom. It was over, he was going to Leavenworth Penitentiary.

Reba Sue and Patsy sat together in the courtroom. Patsy was devastated when the judge read the sentence. Reba Sue sat there pissed off, shaking her head and giving the judge the best go to hell expression she could conjure.

Reba Sue had done all she could to help him, and she had failed. She was angry with Charles. Why had he been so stupid? He had ruined their family and now another family was left in ruins.

Charles turned to look at the two women that he loved. He had disappointed them, and they had stood by him regardless of his transgressions. They were exceptionally loyal and always would be.

THE BIG HOUSE

When Charles arrived at Leavenworth Federal Penitentiary, he had two more court cases hanging over him. He lost his appeal on the Hartford case and was sentenced to twelve years in Cummins Prison Farm in Arkansas. Cummins was one of the most notorious prisons in the United States. There had been many unexplained deaths, and the prisoners were treated harshly. Charles was hopeful he wouldn't have to serve that sentence at the end of his time served in Leavenworth.

He was transported from Leavenworth to the Muskogee Federal jail on July 8th for a lineup regarding the Hartshorne robbery. He hadn't cut his hair since he was arrested for the Carney debacle. It was long and shaggy, and he had grown a beard and mustache. The U.S. Attorney for the district was furious as the woman who saw a glimpse of him during the robbery couldn't identify him. He asked the judge in the case to declare him in contempt of court and to order another lineup. The judge agreed, and in August, Charles came back for another lineup with both head and beard shaved with as much hair as a Marine boot who just entered training camp. She still couldn't identify him.

The courts dropped the charges against Patsy and Jonesy's wife. Patsy was relieved. She had suffered for months, not knowing if she would also end up in prison. After a while, she filed for divorce. Charles understood that she couldn't wait for him, and that she needed to move on with her life.

While Jonesy was out on bond for the Hartshorne indictment, he was caught red handed inside a bank in Chidesier, Arkansas, late at night, cutting through a vault door with a welding rig. He was convicted and sentenced to twenty-one years in Cummins Prison Farm.

As the trial date approached for Charles and Jonesy on the Hartshorne robbery, Jonesy escaped from Cummins. He drove a truck through prison gate and gained his freedom. The trial was postponed, and four months later, the district attorney dropped the charges against Charles. Charles was pleased that he wouldn't have this one hanging over his head and he couldn't believe his buddy escaped Cummins, but anything was possible when it comes to Jonesy Monson. That guy was one brave son of a bitch.

After serving two years in Leavenworth, Charles's conscience for betraying the McGillis boys and Ruthie came to a head. Their father had been one of Charles's best friends since high school, and he had done wrong by him. He wrote a letter to his old friend, saying he wanted to testify before a judge that he was the one who had robbed the Lockesburg bank and would do anything to obtain their release from Cummins prison. They'd been there for two long years. In the letter, he wrote that he was doing this for his peace of mind and that he has hated himself for betraying his friend.

Wiley McGillis took the letter to Arkansas governor, Winthrop Rockefeller and his aide of prison affairs, O.H. Storey, and begged for their release. Storey told McGillis that they had not exhausted their remedies in court. The state supreme court heard their arguments and decided that the search warrants also were not sufficient. The court refused to hear testimony from Charles, but the courts decided to pardon the McGillis boys and Ruthie.

Charles wasn't charged with the Lockesburg bank robbery, and they didn't want his testimony. This surprised him because he was ready to accept it in order to get them out of prison.

A few weeks later, Willey McGillis accepted a collect call from Charles.

"Charles, we got 'em out!"

"Thank God, I'm so sorry, Wiley. I put your family through hell on this."

"I should have gotten them a good lawyer with the money you gave me back then. They released them because the search warrant wasn't sufficient. Can you believe that? They didn't even want to hear from you. And I'll tell you this Charles, if you hadn't written that letter, they would still be rotting in that hell hole of a prison. We wouldn't have gotten in front of the supreme court without you."

"This has been so heavy on my heart for three years. I'll never forgive myself, and I'm sorry. I hope you and your family can forgive me."

"Charles, I forgive you. I can't speak for the rest of them, but I do forgive you. I just hope that once they get out, they aren't traumatized by their time in prison."

The phone beeped in, and Charles knew they had one minute to wrap up.

"Thank you, Wiley. I wish I had come clean on it a long time ago. I'll write to you soon. And please tell the boys and the young lady how sorry I am. Goodbye, Wiley."

"I will do it. Goodbye, Charles."

Charles was settled into prison life. He was a foreman on the construction crew, and, of course, he had a scam going to bring in money. Several of the inmates were artists, and he would have them paint an oil painting, and then he would sign his name to it. He had some woman selling them as Charles Parrott's artwork. It was a sham, but the inmates would get part of the money and that made him plenty of friends behind the bars.

Charles in Leavenworth working in construction

In April of 1973, the FBI captured Jonesy. He was living in Pennsylvania in an Amish community in the Poconos. He'd married a woman there, even though he was still legally married to Peggy. The people in the community were shocked. They knew him to be a good citizen, who was well respected and loved by many of the people there. Jonesy was convicted of the Hartshorne robbery and sentenced to fifteen years in Leavenworth. Once there, he and Charles were able to resume their friendship. Charles assured him that once the statute of limitations was up, he would try to get him out of Leavenworth on the Hartshorne sentence.

His children came as often as Reba Sue could get them to the prison. Susan wrote him letters often, and Charles Lee was sinking into a life of being a troubled teenager and didn't contact him very often. Reba Sue wrote to him about Charles Lee getting shot by the police when he was committing a petty crime. The bullet wound was superficial, and Charles Lee survived. Charles was devasted. He had failed as a father, and he hoped that Charles Lee wouldn't follow in his footsteps. He was as tough and brazen as Charles was in his youth. He now knew the feeling of dread that his parents had experienced with him.

He didn't get to see young Toni Lynne as she grew up. She would never know him and that hurt his soul. He wrote and told Susan to take care of her and to remind her of him, but Susan never responded to that letter. She ran away from home in 1973 at the age of sixteen, and he wouldn't hear from her for over a year and half. When he did finally hear from her, she had married a recording artist named Phil Seymour from Tulsa and was living in Hollywood, California. He was relieved that she was all right and seemed to be happy.

The prison sentence took a lot out of him, but Reba Sue was always there for him. She sent him magazine subscriptions to *Rolling Stone* and *Sports Illustrated* every year. She wrote him often and kept him updated on the kids, even when it was awful news. She would always love him and be loyal to him and it was the same for him.

Slim threw a big party for Charles after his release in 1975. There were a lot of his friends there.

"Hey Charlie, your buddy Lyndal just told me that there's some G men out there taking down tag numbers. You want to go outside and chat with them?" asked Slim, raising his eyebrows and smirking.

Charles rubbed his chin, thinking it over.

"I don't want to ruin my mood. That might make me want to start up the game again with them."

"You were damn good at the game, Charlie."

"Yeah, I loved robbing banks. I really loved it. And I loved fooling with them. Outsmarting the FBI was a big part of the thrill. I wonder if Agent French is out there?"

"Wanna go find out? I'll go with ya," said Slim.

"Nah, I'm going make them keep wondering about me. That'll be fun. If I see someone following me, I'll drive by a bank real slow and look at it. You know sometimes when I pass by a bank, I still think about how I would rob it."

www.ingramcontent.com/pod-product-compliance
Lightning Source LLC
Chambersburg PA
CBHW022046020426
42335CB00012B/561